MUD
BENEATH
MY BOOTS

By the same author:

Non fiction
The Prance of Men

Fiction
Joshua

MUD BENEATH MY BOOTS

ALLAN MARRIOTT

**A POIGNANT MEMOIR OF
THE EFFECTS OF WAR ON
A YOUNG NEW ZEALANDER**

HarperCollins*Publishers*

National Library of New Zealand Cataloguing-in-Publication Data

Marriott, Allan, 1944-
Mud beneath my boots : Private Coley's war / Allan Marriott.
Includes bibliographical references.
ISBN 1-86950-560-3
1. Coley, Len. 2. New Zealand. Army. Expeditionary Force.
3. World War, 1914-1918—Campaigns—Belgium.
4. World War, 1914-1918—Campaigns—France.
I. Coley, Len. II. Title.
940.4144—dc 22

First published 2005
HarperCollins*Publishers (New Zealand) Limited*
P.O. Box 1, Auckland

ISBN 1 86950 560 3
Cover design by Darren Holt, HarperCollins Design Studio
Cover photograph by Australian Picture Library/Corbis
Internal text design and typesetting by Springfield West

Printed by Griffin Press, Australia, on 79gsm Bulky Paperback

Acknowledgements

I would first like to thank the members of my family and my friends who read and discussed pieces of writing and encouraged me to complete the whole, Hazel Lanyon, Melanie Roberts Fraser, Emma Barker, Dave Barker, Arch Campbell, Rodney Routledge, Bob Manthei, Marjorie Manthei, and especially my partner, Gay Sharlotte.

My nephew Oliver Roberts assured me that if for any reason I was unable to complete my uncle's story, he would do so in the style in which it was begun.

I also thank John Veale for providing me with original maps of the Western Front, left to him by his grandfather, Major JPE Veale.

I am indebted to Walter Guttery at Personnel Archives, NZ Defence Force, for his persistent search of records to confirm that Leonard Coley and Leonard Collins were one and the same.

I received invaluable advice from my editor, Anna Rogers, with whom it was so easy to clarify and consider.

And I am grateful to Lorain Day, Commissioning Editor at HarperCollins, and her team for the immediate response to my first draft, and their subsequent support and encouragement.

To the memory of Julia Vitzky,
first known as Juliana Witzke

Contents

Introduction

This is not my story. It is my uncle's. He died in 1968, when he was 69 and I was 24. He was in Foxton and I was in Christchurch. I was not told of his death in time and did not get to his funeral. Although I would like to have been there to tell the world what I knew of my uncle, I realise now how little I then understood about his life.

Len Coley had been a special part of my early childhood. For most of those years he lived in Masterton where I regularly visited from Mauriceville West or Hastings. He sat behind me on his old, brown-red John Deere tractor, his hands over mine on the steering wheel as we drove around the struggling garden nursery that he managed from the 1940s to the 1960s. Today, 50 years later, I can still hear his sudden wheezing and gasping in my ears. He would stop the engine, leave me in charge of the wheel and walk among the rows of plants until he regained control of his breathing. Sometimes, his need for air was so urgent he would disappear suddenly. I learnt to wait. He would return with a joke to tell me.

In the early morning, I would watch him through a crack in the door as he leant over the bowl of water on the bedside table, lathered his face with soap, sharpened the razor on the leather strap and prepared to shave. Sometimes, as he tilted his head and exposed his neck to the razor strokes, he would lean too far and have to sit on the edge of the bed until he stopped coughing. The bedroom door would shut.

I came to understand that his bedroom, and the outdoors, were safe places for him. Even as that young child, I sensed his shame about the noise he made. When I once asked him to explain it, he refused. 'Something I have to deal with, like catarrh,' was all he said. I asked my parents. They told me he had been 'gassed' during the war. At first, I thought they meant the war of 1939–45, in which my other uncles had served, but I borrowed what books I could find at school and discovered chemical warfare. When I first met Len, he had been struggling with his breathing for over 25 years; he would do so for another 25.

I saw less of him as I grew towards my twenties and he became more homebound, but these vivid childhood memories of Len's struggle were a major influence on my stand as a conscientious objector. Yet at 20, I was led to the gates of Burnham Military Camp for compulsory military training. I stayed six weeks and walked out in protest at the New Zealand government's intended commitment of troops to Vietnam. In the few years that followed, Len supported my decision. In the glimpses I had of his life, whether on the battlefields of war or on his personal battlefields, I saw the fighter and the protester — and the dilemma.

As a child, I was also curious about where I fitted with Len, who was married to my father's older sister, Ivy. My father had been born in 1914, so I knew that Len had to have been much older to have fought in the First World War. He was born in 1898 and, at 39, was 13 years older than my aunt when they married in 1937. It was Len's first marriage. He and Ivy were not able to have children, and few of Len's relations remained in contact. Ivy's siblings and their children became their close relatives.

Leonard (Len) was born on 4 June 1898 in Palmerston North, the seventh of the 10 children of Julia and Alfred Coley. The family's circumstances hindered Len's wish for an extensive school education. His early work experiences were as a farm labourer and a contractor with the Public Works Department.

On 13 December 1915, he enlisted in the New Zealand Army. He was 17, though he declared himself to be 20 — as if born in 1895. His New Zealand Expeditionary Force (NZEF) regimental number was 21936. Len also lied about his name, enlisting as Leonard Collins and, for next of kin, writing down his father's name but describing him as an uncle. He was 5 feet 4 inches (162.5 centimetres) tall and weighed 133 pounds (60 kilograms).

Len spent three years and 23 days overseas with the NZEF. He fought on the French/Belgian Western Front at the Somme, at Messines, at Ypres and Passchendaele, and again at the Somme. He was hospitalised, and spent time in training and convalescent camps in France and England. He was, at various times, wounded, concussed from explosions, poison gassed and given up for dead. A crack sniper for his unit, by the time he was 20 he was both younger and more experienced than most of his army mates.

Yet before that birthday he was questioning the war and its impact on his fellow soldiers. He returned to New Zealand in May 1919, shattered, suffering severe loss of health and desperate to forget what he had been through, but had to spend three more months in hospital. When he was discharged, on 14 August 1919, he symbolically kerosened and burnt every piece of his army uniform. Like all those who served on the Western Front, he received the British War Medal and the Victory Medal. The latter is inscribed on the reverse with the phrase 'The Great War For Civilisation'.

Familiar with the terrain of his birthplace in Manawatu and with youthful experience of the West Coast, he disappeared for long periods through the next decade into the bush and farmlands of New Zealand, where he regained some health and strength. He did not talk of these experiences.

In 1930, Len returned to France and Belgium, to walk again in the streets of Armentières and stand in 'Half Past Eleven Square'. He reflected on his years at war. During 1930, drawing on notes he had made and kept during the war, he wrote a comprehensive journal of that time, and of the changes he saw in himself. The journal was written in longhand over many months and clearly checked for accuracy concerning dates and places. He took that journal into his marriage but I have no idea how much of it he shared with my aunt, or with my parents. He did, though, keep his writings, along with newspaper clippings and the official telegram his mother received of his death and the telegram that said he was actually alive.

Len died on 24 April 1968, just before Anzac Day. When Ivy died in October 1975, my parents acquired Len's journal. Surprisingly, they did not tell me of it and I had no idea of its existence. In 2001, after both my parents had died, I was, as trustee, working my way through their estate when I uncovered Len's journal by chance. Although its condition was of concern — it had been casually stored — at least it had been kept.

I have reshaped Len's journal as he described events from 1915 to 1919, and included reminiscences from his return to northern France and Belgium in 1930. I have kept the spelling of places accurate to the time, although many in Belgium have since been changed. Len altered most of the names and ranks of the men about whom he wrote to protect their circumstances. Fortunately, he left enough coded information for me to verify and reinstate correctly where possible and appropriate. Len refers frequently and with strong attachment to Chloride/Snowy Lyford and Lew Stemp: Chloride was Clarence Lyford, of Palmerston North, NZEF Regimental No. 11893; Lew was Henry Louis Stemp, of Wanganui, NZEF Regimental No. 31367. I have left Len's mixture of kilometres and miles, and metres and yards, as he wrote them. And I have written this book, as best I can, using the words of Len (Sonny) Coley.

Allan Marriott
2004

Chapter 1

Armentières, 1930

I know my pilgrimage must begin at Armentières. Even before I arrive, I feel my legs again marching along that Belgian frontier, so near to Lille. It is drab, this industrial French 'West Riding'. It is not a place for an impressionist. But I am here.

The train passes alongside flat, ditched fields, through Chapelle d'Armentières, and puts me down at a new station. Yet it is the old station. It opens on to the same paved place, where the bricks are still small and irregular. I think I recognise the two restaurants at the opposite corners of the Rue de la Gare, the restaurant of the Prophet and the restaurant of the Count of Egmont.

Dusk is deepening. From the cafés and estaminets, I can hear the sound of gramophones. They used to fill the side streets with their noise in 1916. But tonight, something from *Rose Marie* is being played. I forget what was played in 1916. Old dance tunes perhaps, and patriotic marches. The troops at rest sang songs from the *Bing Boys*.

So much still seems as it was, yet there is a French policeman on traffic duty.

Beyond the noises of the streets there is a strange calm, a

stillness even. There is no vibration in the air from guns and no heavy traffic rumble over stony roads. The sky is unlit and empty. The quietness is extraordinary.

'Half Past Eleven Square' is transformed. The stopped clock, which had given the square its name, had stood in the old damaged tower when I first arrived here in 1916. It has gone. There is a new Hôtel de Ville. It has a tower and a clock but it is very different from the old town hall. The façade has been shortened, I am sure of that. It is now a square and compact building.

The red brick Church of St Vaast looks taller. Its spire of white stone, like the old landmark, is fresh. I remember only the ruin. There is a new market hall. Somewhere beneath will be the wreckage of masonry and glass.

I keep staring at the new monument in the Grande Place. It is a white stone obelisk to old Armentières and its dead. This part of the town is rebuilt, entirely, I think.

Yet much seems familiar. It is easy to find my way about. I turn a corner and stop at a well-remembered vista. Old thoroughfares are under old names. The Rue Nationale, the Rue Sadi Carnot, the Rue Denis Pepin are here. Perhaps they are more durable than the material they are made from. Perhaps they were indestructible to obliteration by war.

I stare at new boots on my feet. The roads of Armentières today are still the hard and uneven paved roads of 14 years ago. Some have been renewed but most of the large chips and fractures date from the war. This is the same surface that in 1916 and 1917 made marching for the troops so damn wearying.

Tomorrow morning, I will walk towards Houplines where the trenches had been. I'm not sure how I feel about that.

Chapter 2

Armentières, 1916

It was a beautiful morning, just a faint chill of early winter in the air. We were returning from the Somme, and this was the first that many of us in the 2nd Brigade, NZEF, had seen of old Armentières. It looked so venerable. It gave us all a sense of peace as we entered the town. We needed that. We had had only a few advancements at the Somme. Even with our mixture of new soldiers, Gallipoli veterans and New Zealand doggedness, our battle front had remained basically unaltered. The stunt had tired us.

But as we marched into the square, I was shocked. The only building damaged was the cathedral. The roof was completely shattered with great jagged holes in the walls. The German gunners had made a very thorough mess of it. We entered carefully. All the fallen debris around the altar had been cleared for 20 feet but the altar itself remained intact. The French locals continued to use it for their services, just as they did in pre-war days. I learnt later that they were called to prayer every day by the ringing of a small hand bell. In weeks to come, some of us would join the 30 or so locals who were left. They enjoyed that.

As I turned to leave the cathedral, I saw what had once

been a beautiful and huge stained-glass window. Most of the glass had been destroyed, but in the middle of it a figure about 5 feet high remained virtually untouched, apart from some minor cracks. I felt a strange feeling of awe that the Virgin and Child was mostly preserved given that the rest of the church had suffered. It was almost too reverent for me.

I stood on the steps and faced the town hall. The clock, seemingly unscathed, had stopped at half past 11. For the first time, I was actually seeing what, for military purposes, had become known as Half Past Eleven Square. Turning south, I faced a row nearly a quarter of a mile long of shops and houses. Many had been shelled, others were just a rubble of bricks.

Beyond were the outskirts of Houplines. In every direction there was desolation and ruin as if some monstrous and violent earthquake had imposed itself upon the town. Yet to the east, surprisingly, many of the warehouses on the bank of the Lys Canal could not have had more than three hits. They were so little the worse for wear compared with the wreckage elsewhere. They were clearly used as billets and stores for material. The town was not shelled now and these places were safe.

A mile from the square, we came upon the first of the communication trenches. They led to the front line. The main two were named Cambridge Avenue and Duck Walk Avenue. A hundred yards to the right was the girls' convent. It was totally ruined. We learnt not to ask twice about the convent. The locals, whom we all came to love, could only speak of the convent with bitter hatred in their eyes and a snarl on their lips. The deeds perpetrated by the German soldiers within the convent caused them too much pain.

From here, we looked out over miles of flat country to Lille, a dirty red and orange blur on the horizon. Between, numerous heaps of bricks told me what had once been many farm houses and outbuildings. The countryside was pitted everywhere with shell holes. Here and there, a small bunch of crosses spoke their own grim story.

We were warned not to stand here too long. Machine guns were still trained in our direction, or the occasional whiz-bang from a field gun might hurry us on our way. We gained the shelter of Cambridge Avenue and walked towards the reserve trenches, a quarter of a mile along. Here, several men were stripped to their waist, some slowly running up the seam of a singlet or shirt with a lighted match or small piece of lighted candle as they squeezed the material together between their fingers. Some called out 'What's the news?' or 'How's things in New Zealand?' While we chatted briefly, the men continued to 'read their shirts' or look for body lice. The ground teemed with the parasites. It was impossible to get rid of them while in the trenches. Many of us resorted to shaving our bodies all over in order to gain a little comfort. It was often necessary to do so to prevent eggs being laid under our armpits. It was a continuous process, trying to reduce their breeding grounds on our bodies. I didn't mind shaving. It was easier for me than those with lots of body hair.

The dugouts here were better than many I had already been in. Though there was mud on the floors because it was October, there were duck walks to lie on. Some foragers had even provided themselves with mattresses and a few sacks. It was even possible to keep a brazier burning as there was plenty of fuel handy. It was risky when out collecting, but we all ran risks for the sake of a little comfort. The nights were cold and my overcoat and one blanket did not often keep me warm enough. As everyone had been ordered to, I slept with my clothes on. It was sensible in case we had to turn out at any minute.

The support trenches were another half a mile further on. Mud everywhere was ankle deep. Occasionally, we came across a trench mortar with ammunition stacked in front of the emplacement and protected by the bank in such a way that it could not be hit by shells or shrapnel. If it were, we would all go sky high.

The front line was now only a quarter of a mile away. It was probably the safest place of all from shellfire. It was rarely shelled unless we or the Germans were preparing for a raid. And then it became too lively. Again, the mud was deep but the trenches were laid with duck walks. If they hadn't been, we would soon get bogged if we had to move quickly. The trench showed signs of patching everywhere and was perhaps 7 feet deep in places. Two feet above the bottom of the trench was the fire step that raised us to chest height for firing. The dugouts here were poor and could only be entered on hands and knees. It was impossible to sit upright in many of them. The floors were not only muddy but infested with huge trench rats and the regular parasites.

Our whole division had now arrived. We spent the afternoon drawing rations and preparing to relieve the 2nd Division of Australians who had been holding the line. At 5pm on the 16th we moved up to the front and effected the relief without mishap. There had been machine-gun fire from the Germans but they were shooting blindly in the dark.

I tried to settle immediately to what is often the humdrum of trench life. As this was my fourth time on a front line, I had no wish to bother Fritz unless he bothered me.

A few mornings later, we were all taken by surprise. Unheard by us, the Germans had put up a notice during the night: 'Don't shoot — Saxons in'. They proved their genuineness by openly showing themselves at intervals during the day. We did likewise in daylight but kept a strict lookout as soon as dark fell. As we were only 80 yards away, we were not such fools as to trust them blindly, but they never made any attempt to leave their trenches. Four mornings later, another notice appeared: 'Being relieved at dark by Bavarians or Prussians'.

That night, we faced the Bavarians. We saw a large fighting patrol in no man's land about 1am. We knew we had no such patrol out. One of our machine gunners opened up and immediately killed eight of them. We sent out six men, covered by machine gun, to get badges and papers from the dead men. This information would eventually be sent by our headquarters to Germany. By daylight, the dead were gone, as we had hoped. We would not fire on men collecting their comrades, but none of us on lookout had even seen them removed.

That was probably because of another surprise we got later that night. Fritz introduced a searchlight somewhere near their supports. We guessed it was mounted on a truck on rails. It would appear in several different places, sweep our front for a few seconds, then disappear. It became a serious menace to us in the days that followed. A week's leave to Paris was promised to any one of us who smashed it with a bullet or by any other means. The artillery soon got onto the different positions it appeared at. The moment it showed, guns barked everywhere. It took three weeks before a shell smashed it. Fritz set up the searchlight again, about one and a half miles away. It was too far for any of us.

The morning after the introduction of the searchlight, we were strafed. One high explosive shell landed in a toilet nearby where chloride of lime was used freely. Snowy Lyford smelt the lime and mistook it for gas, its smell being similar to phosgene and chlorine. Snowy yelled 'gas' and gave three hefty bangs on the gas alarm. Masks were grabbed in haste and other alarms rang through the trenches. Although the others near me and I couldn't smell or see gas, we stood ready to slip our masks on just in case. Within seconds, the skipper tore down the trench to find out who had set off the false alarm. Snowy and a mate stood there with masks already on. Snowy's explanation received a father of a tongue banging and he got a week's patrol for his trouble. We called him Chloride after that. He took the chaffing like a sportsman.

We were suddenly reminded that Fritz had had it all his own way since daylight. Some 'ressentiment' was called out for, and our trench mortars came to life among shouts of 'let's give them some presents'. We fired Stokes shells and plum duffs, and a few rifle grenades were thrown in from the front line for good measure. Our compliments were returned with pineapples and minenwerfers, both big and small. They gave our front line and supports a liberal dose, killing two of our men and wounding several. I hadn't known them.

The minenwerfers caused great nerve strain, being as big as an 8-inch shell, and they could be seen from the moment they left the gun. Their only redeeming feature was the time they sometimes gave us to get out of their way. The pineapple, although dangerous, was only as big as an actual pineapple and was a joke beside the minenwerfers in terms of their power. The minenwerfers, at 2½ feet long, could weigh between a half and 1 hundredweight and were capable of enormous damage.

The day quietened and I played cards. Others shot rats by baiting their bayonet with crumbs of cheese and bread and pulling the trigger when the rats nibbled. Others read their shirts or slept.

An hour before dark, we were called to stand to. At exactly the same time, Fritz suddenly introduced their ace of aces among machine gunners. He was so good that peeping over the top of the trench was not worth a try. The way that man handled his gun was uncanny. His favourite hobby was to cut the top of the sandbags of the trench with explosive, copper-coated bullets. We reluctantly admired his accuracy. We were equally keen to remove this one man in particular. He became the terror of the front line for more than two weeks before he was taken out. We were relieved that Fritz had no other man who came close to his accuracy.

At night, we sometimes indulged in a few songs, but it was common to hear music and singing from Fritz's side. Mouth organs, accordions and violins were regular. I was astonished one night to hear a rich, soprano voice from their side. A woman singing in the German front line seemed incredible, but there she was. She had a lovely voice and her presence meant we gave Fritz far more peace than was our wont. For several nights, on her account, we stopped firing our trench mortars as a usual goodnight blessing.

This couldn't go on indefinitely. We decided on a night raid and prepared for it on the days before with intermittent trench mortar fire intended to keep the woman away. Four nights later, half an hour after stand-down, our whole company left the trench in batches of six at a time. We waited in no man's land for orders. Hawke's Bay Company was on my right and Ruahine Company on my left. They were to provide a machine-gun barrage to protect our flanks and keep Fritz down as we attacked. The artillery was to do likewise from the support and communication trenches.

As our troops fired, we worked our way over the ground as close to Fritz as we could. Our trench mortars ceased fire. Our company Lewis gunners opened fire on the run, guns held at the hip by a strap over their shoulder, spraying the top of the German trench. The rest of us had to keep pace. As we got to about 7 yards from the trench, our Lewis gunners stopped firing, dropped to the ground, and we charged. We leapt into their dugouts and trenches, bayonets in front. There was no resistance. The first Germans were dead, caught in our barrage, and the rest had disappeared.

Fritz swung his searchlight on the scene and flares went up everywhere from the German supports. It was suddenly like daylight and easy to see what we were doing. Our officers gave us five minutes in the trenches to clean up stragglers and take any of their walking injured. With two short blasts on whistles, the officers had us heading for our own trenches for all we were worth, dragging 10 prisoners. The German artillery opened up on the wrong line, thankfully, giving us a chance to dive for shelter without any casualties. I had just made the trench when the German artillery corrected its mistake and hit us like a tornado for the next half-hour.

As we kept our heads down, and made no attempt to fire back, I realised what I had just seen in the German trenches. No wonder they held concerts. Fritz had dug in to stay and had not wasted time. I had never dreamed that such dugouts existed anywhere on the whole Western Front.

All the dugouts were 15 to 20 feet deep. A 12-inch shell couldn't have pierced them. Some would have held 20 men, standing upright with room for all and room to spare. In every dugout, there were bunks in tiers of two. There was no mud on the floors and no sign of rats. When I looked around me at our restricted and miserable cubbyholes, I shuddered. I had thought our dugouts here were better than most, but I had just compared comfort with misery.

Our company was given leave for a week and, with my mates, I went back into billets at Houplines on the outskirts of Armentières. I got relief from the mud and parasites but I kept seeing the German trenches.

During the days, we were drilled to smarten and

sharpen us up. In the evenings, dozens of us headed to Half Past Eleven Square and made our headquarters in the two estaminets. Many of the men hoped to meet with one of the girls or, failing that, just to bask in their smiles. Every night, I heard Marie, Yvonne or Marguerite whisper in their solemn accent, 'après la guerre, M'sieur'. I think every one of us had that same promise from one of the trio. In their company, most of us enjoyed a decent, civilised meal of ham and eggs with 'café au lait', followed by beer or cheap wine in the estaminets.

For half a franc per garment, some of the men left parcels of their underclothes for the girls to go over with a hot iron during the slack hours of their day. It was the best method of killing the body lice and eggs. One or two sly dogs had made it big with the girls by collecting and chopping firewood for them and, at night, doing service as waiters. Although we called them cute and clever lads, hundreds of us envied them.

Even getting a smile from the girls had some of the men reward them with presents as a tribute. It was like a comedy of *Antony and Cleopatra*, each man trying to outdo the other in the splendour and originality of the present. It was not surprising that the three girls ruled hundreds of men, kindly, firmly and lovingly, as if they were helpless babies. I could only watch it. Yvonne, especially, smiled at me a lot. She would ruffle my hair and call me Sonny, my nickname on account of my age, but I was too young to try and compete. Not that I would have told the girls that, but I really didn't expect any 'après la guerre' for me.

The week was up all too quickly and I was back at the front line in trench 86. The nights were very cold as winter was on us properly. As I pulled my coat and blanket around me, all I hankered for was peace and quiet. On my third night, it changed suddenly and embarrassingly.

Between 86 and 85 was a gap of about 2 chains, the trench having been completely blown away by the Germans. It was our custom to keep a patrol of two men passing twice an hour from our trench to the other, reporting all okay and then returning. The gap was a favourite place for Fritz to pepper and would have been a good place to carry out a silent raid if they had been so minded. The gap was not well wired as it was constantly swept by machine-gun fire. Their marksmen must have been indisposed on this night, as there hadn't been a single sally. Contrary to usual form, Fritz had not sent up any flares either. As they usually provided the fireworks, we were suspicious.

Chloride Lyford and I were the two patrolling the gap. We had only just returned to our trench when the jam tins containing small stones and fastened to the wire in front of the trench rattled. We had been expecting rain, but it hadn't yet started, and there was no wind. Chloride and I carefully stood on the fire step, poked our rifles over the top and ahead of us. I was tingling all over but determined to deal with whoever was there. I couldn't see a thing in the blackness. I began to imagine huddled shapes in front of the wire.

I grasped Chloride by the arm and whispered to warn those in the next bay that I was going to put up a parachute flare. I waited for him to pass the warning along the trench. I became more and more sure that someone was close to me. Two minutes elapsed, and I fired the flare. It shot skywards, a trail of sparks behind it. It dangled a fraction of a second at its zenith and turned. The parachute opened and floated slowly along no man's land. Everything was lit up for 200 yards. I still couldn't see anyone.

Just as the flare reached the ground, nearly burnt out, I glanced to my right. I went hot and cold. Not more than

2 yards away, lying full stretch and watching me, was a German. For the fraction of a second I saw the reflection of the flare in his eyes. Slowly, so slowly that I hardly seemed to move, I stepped off the fire step drawing my rifle with me, and faced Fritz. I crouched, my bayonet on the spot where I had seen his eyes. I leapt, and forced my rifle into him as hard as I could.

There was an awful scream and startled shouts from my mates. They were still gazing into no man's land and hadn't known that I had left the fire step. I dropped my rifle in shock as I had driven it in too easily. I had expected something but nothing like the scream that rent the air. I rescued my rifle and jumped back into the trench. On my bayonet, it having passed clean through, was a very dead, black cat.

The barracking from the men was pretty fierce. Chloride got some of his own back by continually parodying 'Who Killed Cock Robin?' with 'Who Killed Our Cat?'. Amid their laughter and my embarrassment, some of the men stopped calling me Sonny and renamed me Puss. I was grateful for the skipper giving me credit for my intentions. But I had to bury the cat.

The following day broke dull and calm, but only for a short while. Seven Taubes nosed around above us early in the morning and we were quietly watchful. Suddenly, six of our planes dived on them and began the best air fight I had seen on that front during the time I was there. At first the RAF was on top, then Fritz, then the RAF. With all the bullets flying about, I didn't see how an insect could have lived through it.

After about 10 minutes, two Taubes, together, trembled, side slipped and reeled away into a nose-dive. We cheered but instantly one of our planes crumpled and fell. As it crashed, another Taube heeled over, then another and they hit the ground together. One of ours burst into flames, and the pilot and observer jumped clear. One of the parachutes failed to open. A Taube dived, firing wildly at the man drifting down as he dangled below his chute. Sadly, the last of his fall was in flames. The remaining Germans headed for home.

We saw that one of our planes was in trouble, coming down in wide circles, landing in front of Houplines. I learnt later that the plane had been shot to pieces and that both pilot and observer were wounded. Apparently, the wounded men had just reached safety when Fritz shelled the plane, scoring a direct hit.

Just before we had gone into the front line, the engineers had installed about a dozen cylinders of phosgene and chlorine gas, each buried about 3 feet below the trench for safety. There had not been a favourable breeze for a gas attack during most of my stay until my second day in the reserve trench. Engineers were hurried up the line to conduct operations.

About 10am, I saw the greenish and yellow cloud start on its way. The gas had hardly reached Fritz when the wind changed and spread it along no man's land. By this time, Fritz had put his artillery to work and pasted our front line. The change of wind was not serious, though some of the gas passed close to our trenches on the left. The bulk of it still headed towards Fritz, but not where intended. They succeeded in blowing up two of the cylinders but our casualties were slight. All our men had been taken out of the line so that it was practically deserted.

I spent six days in reserve, and again returned to billets in Houplines. In the morning, we drilled as usual, were on fatigue in the afternoon, and early at night headed for that Mecca of the Diggers in Half Past Eleven Square. The routine became monotonous. Only the smiles from Yvonne broke the boredom. Full winter had set in and it rained continuously.

When I had to return to the front, the locality was changed to 88 and 89 trenches. They were knee deep in mud from days of relentless rain, and the water in the communication trenches was nearly level with the tops of the thigh gumboots with which we had been provided. In some mornings the rain stopped but it started again at dark.

The extreme left of 89 opened on to the bank of the Lys Canal. The canal itself was in flood and the trench was half full of water. One machine gun team and two gunners were the only occupants. We were wet through and there was no hope of sleep, the dugouts being as muddy as everywhere else. I kept thinking of the German trenches I had seen.

The cooks were with us in the front line. If nothing else, we did get two hot drinks of tea a day. Any other cooking was impossible and the conditions got more and more appalling. The bomb boxes had been broken up as firewood for boiling the water to make tea. It was impossible to collect anything but waterlogged wood in the open. Here too, the mud was up to our knees. The only way the cook could keep a fire going was to pour rifle oil or whale oil on it. If it made too much smoke, Fritz sent over a minenwerfer or two. I did not envy the cook his job. It was terrible enough without trench mortar flying around him.

On what was supposed to be my last day in the front line for this trip, the 23rd November, Fritz shelled us for an hour. When the artillery ceased, the trench mortars were fired at us for another half-hour. In all, they made us a departing 'present' of over 30 minenwerfers, and dozens of pineapples and coal-boxes. Our wire had almost completely disappeared and gaps were blown in the trenches in over a dozen places. Through it, we only had a few injuries. I was okay.

At dusk, we were relieved by 2nd Otago. In spite of what

they could see for themselves, we warned them to keep a strict lookout through the night. We knew there would be a raid of some kind as Fritz had obviously been making preparations for it during the afternoon. Otago assured us that not even a rat could enter the trenches unnoticed. We left feeling secure that we would soon have a hot meal and a sleep. I was played out and needed it.

I had just reached my billet and taken off my filthy equipment, when hell broke loose. We were automatically called back into second reserve to wait for orders. They were not long in coming. Within 10 minutes, we were on the way back to trenches 88 and 89, the spot we had left only half an hour earlier.

I couldn't believe what I saw. It seemed that as soon as we had left our trenches at dark, the Germans had left theirs but in the direction of ours. They must have been practically in our front trench when their barrage opened up on our men. They had swept through 89 before the first shells had finished exploding and immediately made in the direction of 88 before our men had even grabbed their rifles.

After all the warning we had given them, 2nd Otago were caught blithely sitting down drinking tea and talking. Not one man had been on guard. Fritz played havoc with them and finally took back only two prisoners. All the men from the two platoons in 88 were either killed or wounded. I hated thinking that anyone deserved such a fate, but I was so angry and so tired that I kept muttering it had been their own damn fault.

It took our company hours of hard work in those horrible conditions at night to bury the dead and get the wounded safely to different dressing stations. The Germans had lost just eight men by our count. The whole sector was affected.

We were given the task to render assistance where

required. Getting the wounded out was the worst. We needed four men and one guide to each stretcher. We had to carry most of the wounded overland as the trenches were impossible with mud and water. The guide had to steer the stretcher-bearers clear of shell holes in the dark. Finally, about 3am, we returned to our billets. I got one cup of tea before bed.

The remainder of my stay on the front line and supports was uneventful, fortunately. We had little artillery support available and there was a shortage of shells. Each gun was allowed only 10 shells per day, and only in the case of a raid or outright attack would it be possible for us to have artillery fire. We had to save every shell possible.

Because it was now so late in the year, we accurately assessed that there would not be another general attack. It was just as well. If we had had to fight for just one more day, we would have been practically powerless at the end of it. I did wonder what might have happened if Fritz had known that.

On the 12th December, we left Armentières and headed for the village of Sailly sur la Lys, about 10 kilometres away. We had been told there were comfortable billets awaiting. I tried to imagine sleeping without mud and rats and lice. Ah, 'après la guerre, M'sieur'.

Chapter 3

Remembering Christmas, 1916

I remember Sailly village as small and ugly in 1916. It still is. It was seen as safe — and probably still is. The village had been within range of the bigger German guns but was seen as too insignificant to bother about. Unlike Armentières, most of the locals continued to live there. Perhaps that was surprising. It boasted only a single estaminet with shockingly inferior beer and wine sold at top prices. I remember that but I don't recognise any more where the estaminet would have been. I feel disoriented. I think I walked or stole a ride back to Armentières or Pont de Nieppe for a night out.

Sailly had one attraction for all of us, though. But again as I stare around me, I can't find the barber-shop. I'm curious to see the owner. She was a giant of a woman, perhaps 50 years old. I learnt to strop a razor by studying her. She would grunt and smack the razor heavily on the strop, her face so serious. Yet I remember her hands were gentle on my neck. She always kept a fine edge on the razor and I don't think she cut me once. We patronised the barber-shop most days. Madam had us wait beside an open fire kept at full roar. She knew how to look after us and with no half measures. Just as well. God, it was so cold in those mornings with 6 inches of snow constantly on the ground.

I walk to the Lys Canal that also passes through the outskirts of Sailly. I can't find the ground where we played football in the snow. There are buildings all along here, now, but they don't look new. Even with the cold, I think most of us started to feel better from the exercise, some drill, lots of sleep, good billets and regular meals. But after a week of enduring heavy frosts and light snow, I remember it rained again. I don't think it stopped for another week. It rained a lot in those months. There probably wasn't much else for the weather to do.

I look west across the canal. About 5 kilometres away would have been the front line of the Cordonnerie Sub-Sector. I can remember the name and I can remember Christmas, 1916. On Christmas Eve we had been marched from Sailly to the front line through the inevitable sheeting rain. All of us were soaked to the skin by the time we arrived. We relieved 1st Canterbury, I think, or perhaps it was 1st Otago, amid a bantering of Christmas greetings, and then were left to it.

The rain stopped on Christmas Day but it still broke bleak and cold. I think we were a pretty cheerless lot, but the telegraphed thoughts from people back home in New Zealand eased that slightly.

Christmas dinner was something I could never forget. It was, well, ice and rubber. It began with bully beef stew, layered with ice, though sort of warm at the bottom, followed by an orange that was frozen. I needed my bayonet to pierce it. Lastly, there was tinned Christmas pudding that we had to thaw. It was like rubber to chew. I was sick, for the first time, at the end of it.

I didn't fight on this front line, but not because of that dinner. Absolute freedom of movement reigned during the weeks of Christmas. It was safe to walk overland back to the support trenches if any of us wanted to. We didn't trouble the Germans and they didn't trouble us. It was too cold to even entertain the idea of shooting to kill or wound. Both sides came and went unmolested. It was wonderful that such a spirit of trust and camaraderie existed under those circumstances. No one broke that faith. I had to acknowledge, though, contrary to our beliefs at the time, that the Germans could be gentlemen too.

A few days after Christmas, I contracted double pneumonia and was sent first to hospital at Estares then to the 3rd Australian Hospital outside Boulogne. When I eventually came to, I thought I had died and was in heaven with the angels. The faces around me were so feminine and charming and white.

The image was destroyed when one of them called me 'baby'. Mary, I think her name was. Yes, Mary Cunningham of Edinburgh, she called herself. Fancy remembering that. But 'baby' indeed. Of course I had said I was 20 when I had enlisted, but there in the hospital, the nurses had recognised I was a lot younger than that. I was still 18 that Christmas in 1916 and still shorter than average.

It was a few months before I rejoined my unit, already in the hills near Messines. That became some of the worst and the best of the war. The tears are still with me and my breathing is tight again.

Chapter 4

Messines, 1917

I rejoined my unit in May. When I met the men, I was stunned. I was brought back to the reality of a war. There were only a few mates left whom I had known. Chloride Lyford burst out of the group of unfamiliar faces and together we teamed up with Lew Stemp, whom I had met on the way back to the line. The three of us became inseparable as we spent each day going to the front line for repair work and general fatigue duties. I didn't talk much about our missing mates. Nor did Chloride, or anyone. We had to move on.

The unit was quartered in the catacombs of Hill 63. Some said it was the safest place on the Western Front, and was known colloquially as Red Lodge. It could hold a brigade and we made the most of what it enabled. From ground level, we descended about 30 feet down a flight of stairs to several compartments, all timbered, each holding a company with ease. There were about a dozen entrances along the face of the hill. Just over from our entrance was a YMCA shack that did a roaring trade, not because it was free, but because it was the only buffet for miles around.

Our dugouts were electrically lit and fitted with air-shafts and a large electric fan in each compartment. The hill was about 800 feet high and so we had nothing to fear while inside. The Germans regularly fired shells in our direction but most burst in the roots of trees around the lower slopes doing only minor damage.

Our sergeant, Sandy Weir, was one who got unexpectedly caught by the firing as we returned from repair work on the front line. The explosion was behind me and I turned to see his forearm nearly severed by a piece of steel. The sergeant coolly and quickly put the butt of the handle of his clasp knife in his mouth, pulled on the blade with the fingers of his good arm and slashed through the remaining tendons. He bent down, picked up his hand and the remaining part of his forearm.

He shook it, and said, 'Goodbye, mate, you've served me well.'

He let me tie a tourniquet on his injured arm and bind the stump. I admired his bravery, and he admired my handiwork. We both fainted.

When I came to, Sergeant Weir was burying his arm where it had fallen.

Whenever our artillery shelled Fritz, I often climbed the hill to get a splendid view of the shooting as we could see for miles around us. On the 1st June, hundreds of us were on the top to watch a daylight raid under the noses of German shelling. About 40 of the 2nd Battalion Rifle Brigade left the trenches wearing steel body protectors that came down almost to the groins in front and rested on the buttocks at the back.

Shells burst in all directions, looking like dozens of small mines being exploded by an invisible hand on some switchboard. Messines Hill was alive with whiz-bang guns giving our front line beans while to the left and behind the hill, heavier guns fired rapidly. Our artillery observers danced for joy as they located several German batteries we had not known existed. We watched our raiding party weave and dodge their way behind the shelling. They returned with four prisoners.

As the German firing gradually ceased, our enterprising artillery observers now directed our firing at the newly discovered German batteries. Just as we descended to safety, we watched two huge upheavals of ground, telling us we had blown up some of their ammunition stores.

Next day, we moved from Hill 63 to camp behind our guns and within half a mile of Romarin village and the Romarin and Nieppe Road. We had just completed setting up camp when I witnessed a unique event. Spread along the road for about 2 miles were 17 observation balloons, all about 4000 feet up. Suddenly, a German plane appeared from nowhere. I had no idea how it got past the observers or hadn't been heard coming. It tore along the line of balloons, its machine gun firing incendiary bullets. One after the other, the balloons burst into flames, the observers parachuting from each. In less than a minute, 15 of the balloons were crashing to the ground in flames. Fortunately, the parachutists drifted away from the danger in a light breeze, although at least one parachute didn't open.

Until the German plane was clear of the balloons, the anti-aircraft guns were powerless. He had no more than six shots fired at him before he was gone as quickly as he had come.

Through the next days, we began to liven up for a coming raid on the 7th June. Our artillery fired intermittently but continuously each day, aiming to blow up more German ammunition dumps and batteries. The German guns were quiet. If any fired, our boys had their range and put them out of action. That made it easy for some of us to stroll over to our batteries and watch the shells leaving the guns, shouting as each shell went on its way and shouting again as each shell turned to fall. If some of my remarks could have eventuated, in one hour there wouldn't have been a German left in France.

On the 4th, the same day as my 19th birthday, the whole battalion marched the 3 miles to le Pont de Nieppe for a bath. The baths, in what had been a large brewery, were on the left bank of the Lys Canal, close to the main road to Armentières. In front of the baths was a sandbag factory where about 100 to 150 French women worked. As a brewery in peacetime it was probably ideally situated, but as a bath-house in wartime it was too close to the bridge spanning the canal. Only one company at a time was allowed in the baths, the rest waiting under the cover afforded by the shops and houses in the main street.

The baths comprised eight huge vats holding 20 men at a time. It was lovely to stand upright in 5 feet of hot water and enjoy being quietly cooked. I forgot lice in the pleasure of it. The soak was all too short.

I had just got out of the vats and was towelling down, and West Coast Company was in the baths sounding like a class of children, when a shell whined over our heads and landed on a barge anchored in mid-stream, 2 or 3 chains above the bridge. The barge sank and the shouting and laughing stopped instantly. We listened for any next shells. The second, third and fourth all landed beyond the bridge, but the fifth landed in the canal right outside the baths.

We guessed that Fritz was aiming for the bridge, but no one risked staying still. We made for our clothes. The sixth shell knocked the front corner off the building and the next landed inside, scattering bricks in every direction. None of us were hit but were in various stages of dress and undress as we rushed into the street. Some had a towel around them, some had one leg thrust into trousers, some like me managed to get on only a shirt. Two more shells landed in the baths.

As we fled for safety, the women from the factory also rushed into the open. Both groups met in the middle of the street. There were squeals, howls, and yells as we all hesitated at which way to go. Some of the men dropped their clothes and bolted, naked, some ended up with their shirt or trousers on back to front, and some sat and calmly pulled on their clothes. I stood dumbfounded, undecided for a moment, before getting dressed with more speed than I ever had in my life. It probably took less than a minute for everyone to be dressed before we all burst into laughter. Where the women disappeared to, I have no idea. They had vanished in that same minute.

We made our way, still laughing, to the northern end of the village to wait for all the troops to gather and march back to camp near Romarin. About half of the local population had remained, most living in the northern end, leaving the centre and south almost deserted around the baths.

Suddenly, several German batteries opened fire. We instinctively knew from the dull roar that the shells would land close by. A few seconds later, a deluge of shells crashed into the village. Unfortunately, Fritz must have seen our troops. Hundreds had been in the street waiting for their turn in the baths and had bolted at the first shelling.

The screams of women and children cut through the air as the shells hit their homes. We dived into the houses to help bring out the locals. We all knew it meant almost certain death if caught inside. For five minutes, the shelling was terrific and incessant while the troops did the best they could.

It stopped as suddenly as it had begun. I peered through the dust around me. It was heartbreaking. There were civilians that none of us had reached lying everywhere among the rubble of their homes. In the village there probably wasn't a man under 65, most of the elderly women seemed to be over 80, many of the women were clearly mothers, and the children ranged from babes to perhaps 13 or 14. Yes, the locals had known the danger they were in by staying, but I just stared at the stricken and quivering bodies of children and their pitiful cries.

Among them, women writhed with anguish. Most ignored their own wounds as they tried to soothe or caress their children. Some women lay still, children clinging to them, crying or shaking them for the comfort of words.

I cursed and cursed to myself at what I saw and my brain was seared with horrible thoughts. I didn't speak them and nor did my mates. We dashed silently and grimly into what was left of the houses to grab sheets or anything that would serve as bandages. We tended the locals with as much speed and care as we could. I had to cut away clothing to get at wounds and initially shrank from doing that with the women. But I had to. There were so many.

Fortunately, four ambulances arrived with doctors and nurses and bandages from the Red Cross team, all that was possible from the Australian casualty clearing station about a mile away. They had heard the shelling and acted without waiting for any order.

I didn't see a pair of dry eyes in that crowd that day. In the late afternoon, we carried the remains of the dead locals to the pretty little village cemetery where we buried them. The toughest for most of us was burying a mother with her arms latched tightly around her shattered baby. We kept them together.

Back at camp, I couldn't rest. All I could see was that awful devastation of the local people. Our troops only suffered injuries and most of those were from shifting rubble. The homes had been hit, not the troops at the end of the village.

I turned to Lew and Chloride and said, 'Let's get drunk somewhere.' They endorsed my suggestion and we returned to the outskirts of the village to find some local wine.

I do not remember returning to camp but we must have helped each other back because that's where we woke up. The three of us nursed sore heads and none of us could eat the breakfast we put our plates out for. While I sat with my head down, the padre, Captain Walls, called me out. In front of the men, he said had a bone to pick with me.

'So you tried to do me out of a job last night.'

I looked around me at several grinning faces. 'What the hell are you talking about?' I asked.

'You don't know?'

'Can't hazard a guess,' I said.

The padre eyed me closely, walked over solemnly and put an arm around my neck.

'You really don't remember last night?'

'No,' I said painfully.

'Well, when you returned to camp with Lew and Chloride, you stood on this table and made a speech.'

'Me? Don't believe you.'

'Oh, you did — in front of all of us. Isn't that right, men?'

There was a loud chorus, 'Yes!'

One of the men called out, 'Go on, Padre, repeat it for Sonny.'

'This was you,' said the padre. He spread his arms to the air and continued. 'Today, men, we witnessed a horrible, horrible act. We saw babies, children, women, old folk, murdered in the name of war. By God, we were all there. We saw it together. We buried them, babies torn to shreds.

Fritz shelled their homes, not us, their homes. I'm calling on all hands to show no mercy to any single German. We will take no prisoners, is that understood? Understood? And now boys, I bless you all. God be with us.'

The men clapped in amusement. For a couple of days, I lost the names of Sonny and Puss, and acquired the extremely doubtful one of 'Padre'. But it made no difference to my hangover and it made no difference to my feelings about a dead woman wrapped around her dead baby.

The remainder of the day was quiet for me, although our gunners occasionally hammered away at Fritz. By the next afternoon, we had begun to draw rations and ammunition in preparation for the move to the front line that night. All rumours were settled when we had stewed rabbit for tea. We now knew the move to the front was going to be big. For some reason, we were always given a final feed of rabbit in such circumstances. Maybe the bosses thought we would get after Fritz with more speed with rabbit inside. I probably would have preferred Welsh rarebit if the cooks had known about it.

I wrote some letters home, to my mum and to my girlfriend, Ina. I didn't know if it would be my last chance or not to do so. Although as each of the other men would have thought, I was confident I would weather the attack.

By dark, I was watching the artillery preparing their support for us. They had lined up battery after battery, so thickly that the guns stood wheel to wheel. Fritz would not have been aware of so many. Half of the gunners had already lined up their targets and were sleeping until zero hour. I felt even more confident with such support.

The bugle call had us fall-in, the roll was called, the men for the reserve were called out, and the rest of us were handed over to the padre. Captain Walls gave us a short service that we followed with a hymn and prayer. The commanding officer told us to get as much rest as possible. In three hours, we would move forward.

Gradually, the guns ceased. Half an hour before zero, it was quiet. The stillness woke me and, for a short while, I lay there talking with Lew and Chloride. We were whistled into action, putting on equipment and inspecting gas masks.

At 11.45pm, we began our first move of 3 miles to the supports that would be our starting position. We had only gone about a mile when a large German flare shell fell on the crest of Hill 63. It lit up the country in every direction. There were thousands of our troops moving up to their respective positions and our guns appeared grim and stark in the artificial red glow of the flare. Above the crest of the hill, I could see a German observation balloon, probably on top of Messines Hill, 3 miles away.

It was as if Fritz had been waiting for our move. I knew we were in for it. Just as the glow from the flare died away, the German artillery opened up with a vicious roar. I knew what that sound contained. We had our gas masks on before any shell had even landed. The breeze was in our faces and if we moved fast enough, with luck, we would be inside the range of their guns, and the shells and gas would fall behind us.

The high explosive shells hit like a thunderous avalanche. The gas shells, discernible by their faint plop as they exploded, were as thick. I instantly realised that there was no mustard gas in this lot. It was the real thing of phosgene and chlorine. I had to be careful not to wind myself in our rush forward. If any of us did that, we would have to remove the mask. It would be a horrible death.

We had scattered before the first shells struck as it would have been madness to stay in marching formation. Somehow, I lost Lew and Chloride in the scatter, and found myself beside Mac MacIntyre. I knew him as a witty colonial Scotsman and was pleased we were moving together. We had been going well, supporting each other to avoid shrapnel and gas clouds when, without a sound, Mac fell full length across me, sending me spinning into a shell hole.

My mask jerked off and I breathed in a whiff of gas before I could adjust it. I didn't cough, so guessed it was not enough to do me harm. Mac was lying on the ground, his mask off. He was holding one hand over his nose and mouth while trying to retrieve his mask with the other. It probably took two seconds to grab his mouthpiece and push it into his mouth, before slipping the mask on properly. I took a couple of deep breaths with him and pulled him to his feet.

'My leg,' he yelled through the mask. 'Left one.'

His leg was hanging by a sinew or two. I had no time to hesitate. I wrapped a tourniquet above his knee and cut the sinews with my knife. I could feel from the damp around me on the ground and on my hands that Mac had lost a lot of blood. I pulled him onto my back and stumbled my way in and out of shell holes everywhere. I dropped him twice, each time falling and losing my mask from my face.

'Mac, I've got to drag you, can't leave you here,' I shouted to him.

I was starting to feel dizzy and had to nearly choke myself to prevent coughing. I paused for a spell and then tried dragging Mac. We took another header into a hole but didn't lose our masks. I slipped mine partly off to try the air. It was still thick with gas. I turned to pick up Mac. He was dead. I was nearly sick over him. I tried to be his padre but felt stupid. I knew I had to leave him and make for fresher air straight ahead.

But like a fool I was disoriented. I had forgotten how many times I had turned. I must have staggered for a chain when I realised I was going back deeper into the gas. I corrected my mistake and pushed on. The thickness of the gas clouds diminished, but I was having difficulty seeing my landmarks. Without warning, I was hit in the chest with a terrific whack. I knew I fell over.

I came to in a gun pit, staring into the muzzle of an 18-pounder. A group of faces sat around me. None of them had masks on and mine was on my chest.

'You're out of the gas, matey.'

The group of grinning Aussies told me the gun was primed, waiting for orders.

'Hadn't expected you, though,' they said.

They sat me up.

'You went out cold. Only a few minutes,' they said.

My right knee was stiff and I could see that my trouser leg had been ripped open. There was a bandage around my knee.

'Just a scratch, matey. Steel splinter,' said the Aussies.

I had felt nothing. I undid the bandage and dabbed on plenty of iodine. I felt sick and dived for the edge of the gun pit. I left a lot of rabbit on the outside.

I sat with the Aussies a little longer to get my bearings. Only a few stray shells were bursting some distance behind. I thanked my benefactors and headed for the front line again, still about 2 miles away. It was nearly 1.30am.

I knew where to go, but still took an hour through spells of dizziness and nausea. I reported in, found Lew and Chloride and threw off my equipment to ease my shoulders.

'What took you so long?' Lew probed.

I didn't feel like talking to them and told them so. But Lew knew how to get me going.

'Think Puss is getting cold feet. He's a bit too silent,' he said to Chloride casually.

'Damn you, just shut up,' I spat back.

'Hey, tell us, Sonny,' they persisted and sat either side of me.

I apologised and briefly told them what had happened to Mac. I lost the rest of my rabbit at their feet.

I felt better without the rabbit until the whiz-bang guns from Messines Hill started firing randomly at us. I got more and more annoyed with the shelling as I desperately wanted some rest. Along with some of the other men, I hurled curses at the German gunners.

'Bloody swines, you'll get it under your tail shortly.'

'We'll blow you to Berlin to meet the Kaiser face to face.'

'You've got one hour left, you baby-murdering swines.'

The comments were stupid, but I had stopped being silent.

From the orders we had been given, we knew that Fritz was in for a surprise shortly. We hadn't even guessed at the magnitude of it. We had been told that for several months, maybe even a year, tunnellers had been digging from our front line for about a mile and a quarter to right underneath the Germans. The aim was to bring the tunnels under the batteries of guns on the hill. These batteries were in concrete emplacements and absolutely safe from our shellfire. The Germans had every reason to feel secure. They didn't know that they were sleeping on top of 200 tons of explosives.

It was this knowledge that we served up as the main course of our curses. We had been told of the one tunnel with explosives wrapped up at the end of it.

Dawn was close. It seemed as if it had become quiet everywhere in our world. As soon as the sky flickered its first line of pink, word was passed along to 'stand-by'. We had 10 minutes to zero. Every one of us knew that everyone else was ready. I could feel that by just watching the men, although we showed it differently. Some were silent and serious, some joked quietly, and some forced a laugh for all the show of good humour at the prospect of what lay ahead.

Lew, Chloride and I smiled a lot at each other, but there was no joy in my heart. I knew that as soon as our move began, I would be thinking of our enemy, looking for traps and machine guns, listening to the different sounds of different shells as we advanced. It was always like that.

It was 3.10am. A terrific roar rent the air as Messines Hill leapt above us. The earth trembled so violently that many of our men were knocked over by the sheer ferocity of it. The shock to us was incredible and we had been expecting something huge. We hadn't expected to see the whole of the hill move. I couldn't imagine what it must have felt like for the Germans who knew nothing of what happened beneath them. We saw them leave everything and flee.

We had been told that one mine would blow up. I couldn't believe what I saw next. Two more mines exploded with as much force as the first. So there were at least three tunnels, all packed with explosives. The sound was unbelievable. Before the earth stopped rumbling, our artillery opened fire. And before the shells struck, our advance began. (In reality, across a curving front of 16 kilometres, 21 mines, containing a million pounds of explosive, had been dug — 19 successfully detonated.)

There was no resistance for the first mile, and no retaliation from the German artillery. Our guns sounded like the rumble of a huge drum and we advanced in unison with it as if out for a walk with no care in the world. It was a strange sort of music in my ears and gave me a sense of security.

An isolated German machine gun fired in our direction

but it was quickly out of action. The German counter-barrage began to strike but it was ragged and did little damage. Most of their shells initially fell behind the fourth wave of our advancing troops. Their machine gun fire started creeping closer and nearly reached us before our first wave overcame a post of three guns. The first objective was gained and the first wave halted.

We passed through them so quickly, but straight away fell into trouble with two more machine guns directly in front. A few of our men near me were hit just as a shell blew one of the guns and the team to pieces. Seeing no hope for himself, the other gunner threw up his hands in surrender in front of me. He just sat behind the gun with no attempt to move even though the muzzle was now resting on the ground.

I expected trickery. I fired a short burst from my Lewis gun directly at him and he fell back. As I drew level with him, I was horrified at what I had done. I instantly realised why he hadn't moved. He was strapped to the gun by a chain around his wrist and around the tripod. No prisoners, I had said days earlier, and no prisoners now, I said again. I had to keep moving but I did not like what I had done. I knew I had used my gun as vengeance. He may have been a good man.

We had moved so quickly inside the German range, that it took them some time to shorten their fire. The barrage dropped to about 200 yards ahead and was thick with plenty of big shells among it. They probably aimed to prevent us ascending the Hill, now only 300 yards away. I could see lots of German troops ahead but we continued to advance rapidly. Machine guns opened up around us, but we would quickly take them out. Most fled in front of us and made easy targets as they did. I didn't see any get away. Some threw up their hands in a form of surrender, but they suffered the same fate as those fleeing. There was no stopping what we did to them in our advance. We were moving too fast to think about feelings and prisoners.

Lew gave me a spell with my gun. The barrel was getting very hot and the sweat was pouring from me. The German barrage was thinner and still fell ahead of us. I was thankful for the accuracy of our gunners as we had now begun our climb of the steep slopes. We needed all the artillery support we could get from here.

It was almost too easy. By the time we reached the brow of the hill, the German barrage had lost its terror for me. Our fire had been so thick that we passed through the German guns on top of the hill with very few casualties.

Messines village, just ahead, was a smouldering heap of bricks. We took a short rest before again moving forward towards it. Lew and Chloride were still with me. I had gone only about a chain, when I felt my head hit with a terrific whang. I staggered a few yards, fell on my knees and lost consciousness.

I don't know how long I was out for, but when I came to I was alone and lying face down. I raised my head and could just see what was probably the fourth and last wave of our men passing through the remains of Messines village. There were no men behind me. My Lewis gun had gone. They would have needed it. But I couldn't believe they had left me here.

My head throbbed and the right side of my neck was caked in drying blood. My left leg ached. I tried to get up and yelped. I had taken another piece of metal in my calf. I never dreamt I would get hit twice. It was a decent-sized flesh wound. I bound my leg and washed my neck from my water bottle, emptying it. There would be plenty of water from the bottles of dead mates and dead Germans. I began to feel better from cleaning myself up.

There were lots of dead Germans around me. I robbed them of Luger pistols, watches and some badges and, of course, chocolate from their rations. I was hungry and did not fancy our hard biscuits when I knew there were pounds of chocolate lying there, waiting to be collected. I selected three Lugers, six badges and eight watches to go with several pounds of chocolate.

I checked the men spread over the ground around me to make sure there were no other wounded needing attention. There weren't that I could find. I refilled my water bottle, collected two more and left my watering hole.

Way ahead of me, I could make out the stretcher-bearers. So, apparently, I had been left for dead too. I chuckled quietly. Some of my mates would be in for a surprise when I caught up with them.

The day was now very warm and I was beginning to feel the effects of the gas I had inhaled in the night. I had to stop often. Suddenly, I was on the edge of two of the craters blown out by the tunnelled mines. They were huge and capable of holding two or more houses each. Large blocks of concrete and the scrap iron of whiz-bang guns littered the nearest crater to me. I could see German bodies beneath the carnage.

I ambled on, painfully, as my leg hurt, my head throbbed, and I had to pause to breathe properly. I wondered how Lew and Chloride were. I could picture Lew behind my gun, giving the Huns all he could, while Chloride fed him with ammunition at top speed. Both would be doing their best to exact the price of my supposed death in as many bodies as they could. I had got to know both of them so well. They would avenge my death to every extent of their powers.

'Revenge . . . that's what it will be . . . and it sums up the whole war . . . and that's what makes it so bitter.' I could hear myself talking aloud as I walked clumsily on. 'Mates avenging mates . . . that's what keeps us going . . . and if it wasn't for that . . . not half the glorious deeds done, not half the overwhelming victories, would happen. That lust for vengeance drives us on for more blood . . . even when our soul . . . our whole being, is revolted by the sights we see and by the inhuman cruelty and misery of it all. God knows how many women in Germany I've made widows or sorrowing sweethearts today. Yes, I desired revenge too. How many men did I slaughter who could — no, should — have been taken prisoner?'

My words rambled out but I meant them. I walked over body after body. There were so many. 'How many men did my mates slaughter who should have been taken prisoner? But isn't that what I wanted? A price to pay? Dead Germans? By the fieldful?'

I wondered who would agree with me. And I wondered who would disagree. I think I had learnt that soldiers with any experience of this war would say that there was a bond that bound us together. And yet none of us could explain that bond. But I couldn't have seen Lew or Chloride killed or maimed for life and stayed passive. That would have been contrary to my nature. It was like a savage instinct, as if a beast, to hurt those who were to blame for the death of mates. I knew that feeling in me and I realised that the battlefield was the place that gave rein to that desire to give pain. Our inhumanity to each other makes countless thousands mourn.

My aching head was full of such thoughts as I plodded wearily along through the late morning heat. I reached the first field dressing station about 11am. My head and leg wounds were bathed and wrapped before I set out again to try and catch up with my unit.

My pace was slow enough but I came to a crawl when I reached a spot where our men had been shelled by gas. I shuddered. Dozens of still, bloated forms lay everywhere. I had to plod on through them.

I soon came to the 3rd Australian CCS beside the road that led from the Romarin Road in France. I was glad to lie down among the many others also waiting. The heat was terrific and most of us gasped for breath from both that and the partial gassing we had suffered. It took about two hours for my turn. My wounds were not bothered about. I was taken into a tent and given oxygen. I was told I looked green and about done in. I didn't disagree. My lungs felt raw and on fire. I must have gone in and out of sleep and consciousness for the next three days as I was fed oxygen. Every so often, I could dimly see a white-haired old lady offer me cocoa. I do not remember taking any. I just wanted to be left alone.

Someone persistently asked me for my identity disc and kept looking around my neck. Many of us didn't hang them there. It was too gruesome trying to remove them from mates. I said it was tied to the left shoulder strap of my tunic. I was shown only two ends of string. My disc had to have been taken when I was on Messines Hill. I hadn't even missed it. And in the tent, I felt beyond caring.

Later that night, along with several others also receiving oxygen, I was taken by truck to Bailleul, back into France. We were put aboard a hospital train headed for Camiers and the 22nd British General Hospital, near Boulogne. So much for my advance into Belgium. I had now gone in the opposite direction.

I began to feel better as I lay on the hospital bed, but two images haunted me. As we had left the CCS, I had woken up enough to see and hear a huge German sergeant, clearly shell-shocked, screaming like a lunatic as his hands were tied behind him around a tree. I got no peace from watching that. And I worried about my identity disc.

I wrote to Lew and Chloride the next day and told them where I was. I had no idea if they were alive or would receive my letter, but I trusted that our units did their best to get such information through. I received a reply a week later. They told me I had been officially reported killed. I knew what that meant.

I was out of bed like a shot. I found a doctor, explained and got him to cable my mother in New Zealand. I slept, more peacefully, for a few more days.

Chapter 5

Hospital and Training Camps, 1917

The most powerful wireless station in France was just a few kilometres south of the hospital in Camiers. The British Army base camp at Étaples was only 4 kilometres north. Their training grounds bordered the outskirts of the hospitals which themselves covered a good 2 miles square. The main railway ran alongside the front of the hospitals. A few chains to the east of these lines, the main ammunition dump for the whole of the British Army was sited. The dump held everything from .303 rounds to 15-inch howitzer shells.

Not surprisingly, the Germans flew bombing raids over the area nearly every night in an attempt to first destroy the wireless station, and then the dump. To do so, Fritz crossed over the hospitals. Our anti-aircraft guns, which were everywhere, naturally pelted the German planes for all they were worth. Occasionally, a plane was hit. Usually, Fritz was forced back before he got to the wireless station. When he had to turn away, he headed for the railway line and the ammunition dump to give them a try before going home. This nightly activity explained the deep trenches dug everywhere that I had seen when I arrived at the hospital.

Most of us in hospital dreaded the night as it approached.

It was full of unpleasant possibilities if any of the hospitals were hit. I had been in Camiers a couple of weeks, when a German plane was hit right above us. We all thought the pilot retaliated when he dropped his bombs on the 18th General, close by, with obvious havoc. He landed safely nearby and was immediately taken prisoner. The British guard had to fight back a dangerous mob of us. We wanted that pilot. He stood in front of us in a terrible state, crying with heavy sobs.

He took us all by surprise, when in near-perfect English through his sobbing, he gave his account of the incident.

'Four searchlights . . . have me in their beams. Your anti-aircraft guns . . . pelt me unmercifully. It must have been plain to see . . . I am winged and out of control. I have to land. I try to get away from your hospitals to the right. I am driven back. Your gunners will not leave me alone . . . but I am already helpless. Any second . . . a piece of shell might hit the bombs I carry. So, in self-preservation, I release them. I try to miss your hospitals. I dive and land safely. Perhaps . . . if your guns leave me alone, this will not have happened.'

The pilot was so badly affected and distressed that it took him several minutes to get through his explanation. We realised a truth in what he said and felt he had vindicated himself. We didn't touch him and let him be marched away a prisoner.

No wonder these hospitals were unpopular places and our nerves uncontrollable after a few days. Shellfire, no matter how heavy, is still easier to deal with in comparison to aerial bombing. I had learnt to mostly judge where shells could land by their sounds. I found that impossible with bombs. In addition to the effects of the gassing, I suffered from an awful feeling of suspense that I can only describe as physical and mental doubt.

I watched the noble and brave nurses in those trenches at night being subjected to these perils. They always appeared so calm and insisted that the patients took shelter first. Yet I came across them on their own, trembling too.

After a few weeks at Camiers, I was transferred to a convalescent camp at Cayeux-sur-Mer, at the mouth of the River Somme. I was pleased. Cayeux was a pleasant little town and the people friendly. The camp was about a mile and a half away. It was huge and held about half a million men when filled. For nearly two months, I was exempt from all parades except the Monday morning muster. I had the rest of the week to myself. I was still very troubled with my breathing from the gas.

The whole British Army was represented here at Cayeux, right down to Indian and West Indian troops. The Canadians played baseball, and the English, Aussies and New Zealanders played rugby and association football. Because many of us needed time out, cricket was the most popular game — it was less strenuous. Two-up and crown and anchor were always on, but most of the Tommies preferred housie. It suited their pockets best. The difference of pay between the Tommy and the colonial troops was a never-ending source of bad feeling. Whenever the Tommies spoke to us about their small pay, it was with resentment. We were sorry for them and often helped in small ways without hurting their pride. I was good enough at two-up to sometimes deliberately lose to a Tommy. Yet I did not like any of the British guards I met. They had become instantly unpopular from letting us down badly at Flanders. We never forgave them and abused them on sight.

Hundreds of us who were exempt from parades spent much of our time swimming and sunbathing on the beach. I practically forgot I was in a war. Only once, on those lovely afternoons, was our peace disrupted. A submarine rose for a peep at us. We expected shells and scattered. A few shots from the guns at Cayeux soon made it disappear.

One day, I intended to buy some bootlaces from a local shop. In my best French, I asked for a pair. The woman did not respond to my request. She just stared hard. I fished out my French–English guide and pointed out what I wanted. From across the counter, she brushed the book aside and stared harder. I got flustered and headed for the door. She stopped me with 'Non', came around the counter and towards me. I stood with one hand on the door-knob as if to bolt.

She quietly asked me, 'Are you Sonny?'

I hadn't heard that name from a woman since leaving Armentières. Only three women knew it, but I could not recognise her. I stared, bewildered. She turned to a back room and shouted.

'Marie, Yvonne, here is Sonny!'

I recognised them immediately. So the first woman was Marguerite. But she had changed so much. She was older and thinner.

I had never expected to see these three again when I left Armentières. Their closeness to the front had eventually got too much. Our reunion was a happy one and an occasion for a feast. I became very excited and pleased to be with them and eat with them. It was my undoing. I suddenly felt faint and pitched out. The gas had got me again, as it did on other occasions when I was excited.

I came to, lying on a bed in one of their rooms where they had carried me. Yvonne was bending over me, wiping my face, looking anxious. I began to apologise but knew what was coming. I dived for their backyard and once more left a good meal outside me. I returned, feeling pretty seedy, and had to lie down again. I told them it was gas.

The women asked me to stay with them for a day or two until I improved. I explained that I had to be back in camp by 9pm. Yvonne took matters into her own hands. Without saying anything to me, she got out her push-bike, rode over to the camp, told them what had happened and returned with a doctor. On her promise to look after me, the doctor, good sport that he was, said I could stay for three days.

I was so relieved. I got up as usual each morning and helped around their house and shop. I met many of their friends during the day but they would not let me outside until I was ready to return to base. I continued being a frequent visitor while at Cayeux. Yvonne and I spent a lot of time together. We walked the beachfront, sat by the flagstaff on the hill above the sea and rode bicycles out to the heads of Baie de Somme. I felt close to her. I began to wonder if I was in love. She even said I should stay there and marry her.

The idea had its moments to be sure, but there could certainly be none of that until 'après la guerre'.

And within a few days of Yvonne suggesting that idea, I was on my way back towards Camiers, to the British Army base camp at Étaples, in preparation for a return to the front.

Étaples was a fair-sized village, but cheerless. Because its chief occupation was fishing, it was smelly and never looked clean, even after heavy rain. Leave was granted to all ranks every evening. We took it, not because of anything offered in the village, but for the opportunity to mix with other troops and discuss our respective countries over a drink together. We avoided the locals, most of whom I thought untidy, money grabbing and unfriendly.

The camp was large, holding half a million fighting troops in wooden huts and canvas tents. The training grounds, known as the bullring, were at the south of the camp and bordered the hospitals. Only a belt of pine trees separated the tents and the hospitals. The New Zealand camp was at the extreme north with the Australians.

We were bordered by the Portuguese, known to us as the Pork and Cheese. Their camp was totally surrounded by a high barbed-wire fence. They were only allowed leave in limited numbers, provided their behaviour was good. It was necessary. The Portuguese used their knives too freely at the slightest provocation. Previously, a group of Aussies had been badly slashed, three being killed outright and two dying from wounds. The Portuguese sentries, usually on guard with rifle and bayonet, were the only ones in their whole camp allowed ammunition. This was rigidly checked and handed to the 'new guard' when they took over.

The Portuguese were supposed to have had their knives confiscated but they could buy them anywhere from any of the troops who had one to sell. Some made a regular business of it as it provided ready cash. I thought it a very mean game to be in.

It was a march of 2 miles from the camp to the training grounds, six days a week. No matter how much experience any of us had had in battles and no matter what any of us had been through, we were all treated as new recruits. We had to go through the whole works from bayonet drill to gas drill. Most of our instructors were Tommies. Most of them fitted the irascible sergeant major I had often read about. As the colonial troops, we were the despair of their lives. We would not put up with any nonsense. If one of us got into trouble, we all did. We gloried in it and the instructors cursed us for it. The poor, underpaid Tommy troops never dreamt of answering back as we did. For all that, we worked well together. We let the instructors know when we admired them as masters of their art. I found some fine men among them.

Even with our experience, we had accidents at the bomb throwing pits or someone lost their nerve going through the gas mask testing tunnel and was brought out dead. Invariably, someone would pull his mask off in the tunnel, accidentally or in panic, and wouldn't hold his breath for the few seconds required to reach fresh air. Sometimes, our officers were put through their paces by a peppery sergeant major. It did us ordinary privates good to know it and see it. I smiled that we could answer back. The officers dared not if they valued their commissions.

At four each afternoon, there was a general parade followed by the return march to our camps, headed by our bands. With the furthest to go, we New Zealanders were always last to arrive and first to leave. The evenings were a mixture of cards, games and walks. On the Saturdays, we went route marching, to Paris Plage, or into the country behind the camp where we discovered a few secluded estaminets. They were out of bounds but some of us contrived to spend time there. Good booze was hard to find elsewhere.

Paris Plage, right on the sea, was clean, popular and easily reached by tram-car. We required a special pass for this treat. Each weekend, only a limited number of us were granted leave in strict rotation from the full waiting list. It was worth waiting for. Apart from the shopping and the bathing, it was a pleasure to talk to the friendly locals who always seemed interested in us and not bent on money grabbing like others we had met.

I returned from Paris Plage one Sunday evening and ran into the edge of a riot at the railway bridge near Étaples Station. Coo-ee calls filled the air. I knew instantly that the Aussies were calling for assistance from their mates and us New Zealanders, but I couldn't get within 300 yards of the bridge. The place was crowded with cursing and fighting troops of all sorts. Twice, I heard wild yells that sounded serious.

When I reached camp, dozens of Aussies were already there talking it over. By the look of them, they had been in the thick of it. Apparently, earlier in the evening, some of them had met up with a Scottish Victoria Cross winner. The Aussies had poured the drink into him and made a great fuss of his exploits. Pretty drunk, the Aussies escorted the Jock back to camp. They reached the railway bridge when two military police, red caps, asked them not to be so noisy. A red cap sergeant appeared and showed off his authority by ordering the arrest of the lot of them, eight in all. The two private red caps were no fools and tried to argue the sergeant out of his decision. Unfortunately, the sergeant was one of those thick-skulled, overbearing and absolutely detestable men who saw things only his way. He was utterly devoid of tact. He had given an order and now meant to see it carried out. The two privates refused to do so. They obviously scented the danger in the situation.

The sergeant bellowed at them for refusing to obey his order. He insisted the drunks all fall in, with the two red caps falling in behind. No one moved. Mad with rage and before anyone could stop him, the sergeant drew his baton and brought it down on the head of the nearest drunk to him. The man's skull was smashed with the force of the blow.

Being a drunk Australian was not a reason to be interfered with. But it was their guest, the Scottish VC, who was smashed to the ground. Three new red caps arrived as the Aussies picked up the sergeant and threw him over the parapet of the bridge onto the railway line, 20 feet below. He was killed instantly.

The new red caps tried to defend their sergeant. They were also pitched over the parapet, one being killed and one dying from injuries later, as we learnt. The third was terribly handled, punched and kicked from head to foot. The two original red caps also suffered injuries. The trouble was accentuated further by other red caps who reacted to what they saw as an injustice and took to the Aussies. A general fight ensued for a few minutes before everyone cleared out as armed pickets were rushed to the road on the camp boundary and along the bridge.

I couldn't believe that one overbearing, thick-skulled idiot had brought this about when a little tact was all that was required. And a Jock with a VC had lost his life 100 miles from the war front, simply through exuberant good fellowship from a group of Aussies.

All leave was cancelled for 24 hours.

Life in camp was very quiet over the days that followed. Even in wartime, such actions took time to pass over. The dry canteens had fewer patrons, and although the canteen ladies asked no questions, their eyes spoke volumes of concern every time they looked at us. The wet canteen was busier. It served as a sort of relief shop, but the usually noisy conversations were now all in subdued whispers. I think we all felt that while the sergeant got what was due to him as ordinary, common justice, the rest was absolutely uncalled for. The whole event was obnoxious.

Our activities almost returned to normal. It seemed that many of the troops preferred the precincts of the camp to the trip to the village. This did increase attendance at the large wooden picture theatre in the centre of the camp. It could hold about 800 men and boasted a good orchestra. Some evenings, different bands played for an hour or so in one of the camps. These were always very good and attracted plenty of listeners.

Often on a Sunday afternoon, men would visit the

hospitals at Camiers to see mates. If we took a shortcut along the railway lines, we passed the compound, or gaol. It was surrounded by a high barbed-wire fence, outside of which were armed sentries. We could see offenders doing shot drill. This consisted of placing a leaden shot, weighing 10 pounds, in front on the ground, standing immediately to attention, bending, picking up the shot, placing it at arm's length on the ground, taking one pace forward to stand in front of the shot, and performing the operation all over again. After an hour of this, the offender got a five-minute spell, standing strictly to attention.

An offender would be given two buckets of sand, one in each hand, and made to walk at a fast pace before finishing up at the double while going round in a circle the whole time. To relax the man, physical drill would follow, repeated by a smart double round with the buckets again. He would then be put to cleaning salvaged equipment, followed by pack drill done at the double. To vary this, the man would be told to fall in in fighting order. He then had to pull all his equipment to pieces and put it together again, over and over.

If any offender rebelled at these drills, he would be tied to a gun wheel for an hour, no matter the weather, no matter if it killed him. In the evening, he had to 'pick oakum', making loose fibres from picking old ropes to pieces. If he spoke to another offender, he was tied to the gun wheel for an hour. If he reported sick and the doctor insisted the offender was 'swinging the lead', he would be made to embrace the gun wheel. If he tried to stay in bed claiming he actually was sick, he was bullied and treated worse than any dog I have seen.

It looked and sounded like hell in that compound. Many men broke down under such treatment but the rules were always held to. It was surely a peculiar way to make us love our King and country and burn with the fire of patriotism.

A very different and popular attraction was the group of children known as the 'chocolate girls'. They ranged in age from 10 to perhaps 16 and, always escorted by a band of smaller boys and girls, arrived daily from Étaples to sell chocolate to us. Their hours were long, from dawn to dusk. Some of the older girls would follow us for miles on our route marches and, at each halt, would sell their wares. There were some pretty girls among them and some hard cases. They were proud to walk arm in arm with us and chatter away as fast as they could. Wisely, they were careful on whom they bestowed their favours. They soon got to know one and all very quickly. The younger girls would greet each newcomer with 'bisque' or 'bully biff'. They generally got the biscuits or bully beef if the men had it to give.

I enjoyed seeing the delight with which the girls received these presents. If by any chance, one of the men produced a tin of condensed milk, their delight was boundless and their thanks sincere and profuse. The girls were not, and did not even look, starved or hungry, but these items were delicacies to them, poor kids, as the chocolate was to us.

These children were the only popular ones among the whole population of Étaples. The individuality of the adults was crushed by their desire for money. They did not seem able to find the time to keep themselves clean and tidy in case someone got ahead of them in the money-grabbing stakes. I never found this easy to deal with. And God, did some of us know about difficulty with cleanliness and tidiness in the trenches.

The Women's Army Auxiliary Corps, the WAACs, had their base alongside us. The women were chiefly employed driving and maintaining the ambulances and cars. I often found it queer to see a smiling young 'Miss' crawl from under a car, in overalls, covered in oil and grease, or working among the engines with greasy cotton waste in one hand.

They were efficient, to be sure. They had dozens of cars to keep in order as well as the work entailed in maintaining a large garage for such a fleet. I knew they had other duties but the cars and ambulances were their chief care. And who knows, perhaps their chief worry as well, given the demand on the vehicles in horrible conditions.

When convalescent time at Étaples was considered enough, I was sent with a group of other New Zealanders by train to Lottinghen, about halfway between Bologne and St Omer. The journey was tiresome. We were continually held up by traffic heading directly to the front. About 40 ammunition trains, not to mention other classes of traffic, had right of way over us. What should have taken us less than two hours became a day and a half. I was glad to get out of the train. I damned all trains in general and this one in particular.

It came as a pleasant surprise to us West Coasts and Wellingtons when we were told that the brickworks about 600 yards away was to be our home for a few days. We had expected another 3-kilometre march at least. Both the station and, a kilometre away, the village, or hamlet as it really was, each housed the inevitable estaminet and store.

The weather was glorious. It was nearing the end of summer and the whole countryside looked lush. The village was fringed with trees, and with the flowering gardens, the ploughed fields and the late ripening crops of oats, it was picture beautiful in the extreme.

Our billets were comfortable and I was suddenly contented. The locals were so decent towards us, we bought extra vegetables from a fund we each subscribed to for that purpose. The cost was small and the response huge.

Behind the brickworks was a large pond that we used as

a swimming bath. The rest of the battalion were quartered closer to the village, leaving us New Zealanders quite isolated, but with more freedom. Our parade ground was across the road and with everything so handy, we were certainly envied.

We immediately made a start on our special training. New tactics were employed to teach us the Gravenstafel Stunt, or diamond formation, for attack. The idea was that each platoon allocated a section at each point of the diamond, as in the pack of cards, so that we moved forward as a series of diamonds. It may have been a grand scheme in theory, but in practice, we found nothing to recommend it. It was eventually abandoned for the old practice of extended order. Because Gravenstafel was a village near Ypres on the front, this stunt probably meant that was where we were headed.

Towards the end of our stay, the whole division was taken on a surprise 10-kilometre march. We were met and inspected by Sir Douglas Haig and Winston Churchill.* Sir Doug did not strike me as an awe-inspiring Commander in Chief. He looked well on his charger and had a calm dignity, but his square set jaw and deep frown suggested he was trying to look impressive — there in body but not in mind. As I watched the expression on his face, I thought that if he had said to me, 'Double up there, or I'll kick you in the pants,' I would not have been surprised.

The more outstanding parade here involved the battalion. My view was certainly influenced by the fact that the central figure was an old platoon mate from camp in New Zealand. The battalion was drawn up in a large square. In the centre, the colonel sat squarely on his horse. Beside him, three paces

---

* Sir Douglas Haig had become Commander in Chief of the British Expeditionary Force in December 1915. Winston Churchill had been First Lord of the Admiralty, but after the disaster of Gallipoli, for which he became the scapegoat, he had joined the British Army in France. He was then Minister of Munitions.

away, stood the most embarrassed man I had ever seen.

The colonel said, 'Men, I am proud beyond words to have you all here today, and proud of the man standing on my left for being the man of this battalion to bring such distinction upon himself and us.'

I did not actually know what the colonel was driving at, but I was getting an idea because of the situation.

The colonel calmly surveyed us, dramatically, before proceeding. 'Men, I have the great honour to introduce to you, Sergeant Leslie Andrew, now VC.'*

Though I was starting to half expect this, the actual announcement took my breath way. The CO began to call for three cheers. His voice was drowned in our cheering as we shouted out to Les from all sides. It was the loudest congratulations I have ever heard.

The CO's horse got such a scare that it nearly dumped him. The cows in the paddock nearby took to their heels. When the shouting had ceased, the CO read to us the deed and the circumstances that had gained Les his decoration.

Les had performed his deed at Warneton, just east of Messines, during the advance I had been involved in. Eye-witnesses told me that Les had fully deserved his recognition. I had missed it all. I had been dealing with the little lot I had got and was lying in hospital, out to it.

I was proud to know that I had been a mate of Les when in camp, as I had been proud to know Colonel Freyberg,† whom I always thought of as a great soldier, when he had been a dentist with a Mr McKenzie in Levin up to 1915.

Somehow, after the parade, Les suddenly disappeared. We were unable to fête him in person as we wished to.

---

* In the Second World War, as a lieutenant colonel, Leslie Andrew commanded 22 Battalion. He was revered by his men.

† Wounded nine times during the First World War, and awarded a DSO, Bernard Freyberg headed the New Zealand Expeditionary Force during the Second World War.

But in his absence that night, he was the toast and topic of conversation for us all. Les was quiet, unassuming and serious-minded. He was just the sort of man to feature in the role he had.

We left Lottinghen and began our march towards Ypres. The weather was scorching hot, but we were expected to cover 20 miles a day. Even though all of us were in the pink of condition, the march tired us sorely. The cobblestones of the roads nearly crippled me. I had got used to easier going in open country and my feet had become soft.

At the end of the third day, we stopped at billets in a farm large enough to take the whole battalion. My feet were sore and blistered. My shoulders were chafed from the straps of my gear and I was caked in dust from head to foot. My tongue was like a lump of leather. And Ypres was still some distance away.

What I needed, what we all needed, was water to drink and water to wash over ourselves and bathe our feet in. Packs were thrown off, out came soap and towels in all directions. Like a swarm of bees, we rushed for the pump in the middle of the farmyard. There was only room for some at a time and I had to wait my turn.

There was a yell behind us from the farmer. He was clearly annoyed as he shouted several remarks at us about thieves and swine. It suddenly dawned on us all what he meant. We stood back from the pump and politely asked him where we could get water.

'In the village' was his curt reply. That was a mile away. The idea did not appeal to any of us. We had marched far enough that scorching, dusty day. We tried to persuade him. He wasn't changing his mind. We began to argue with him. The farmer removed the handle from the pump and held it in front of us while he continued to argue.

We asked him to put the handle back. He refused and waved it at us. One of our men grabbed it. Startled, the farmer made no move for a few seconds and stared at our man. The farmer suddenly flew at him, only to meet a solid swing to the side of his jaw. The farmer yelled in German-Belgian fury for our officers to intervene. The officers ignored him, their sympathy clearly being with our need for water. The farmer backed away, as if beaten, and returned inside to his house.

We finally had all the water we required. Another of our men removed the handle from the pump. The farmer suddenly reappeared, grinning broadly and apologetically. He reached for the pump handle as if he would be given it. Some of the men laughed at him and mocked him. The farmer reacted with violent rage, swinging his arms everywhere. I thought he was about to have a fit, but he retreated again to his house.

The next morning, before leaving, our troops again washed and drank from the pump. After everyone had finished, the pump handle was ceremoniously dumped down the well that must have been 25 to 30 feet deep. Several of the men got carried away and threw their rubbish down on top of the handle. It didn't take long and the well was thoroughly choked to water level. The farmer stood there pleading pathetically for them to stop. It was useless.

Half an hour later, we were on the march to the village. As we left the farm, I could see the owner standing there, cursing for all he knew, with tears of rage on his face. What surprised me most of all, though, was seeing his wife standing framed in the open window. Her face was wreathed in smiles and, above the sound of our feet, I heard her shout out 'good luck' and 'goodwill' several times to us.

What we had done in filling his well with rubbish was unnecessary. But evidently the way we had treated the farmer met with the approval of madam. I was glad for her sake and hoped there was a lesson in there somewhere.

When we arrived at the village, we were quickly crowded into lorries. We were unloaded about 3 kilometres south of Ypres. Once again, we were expected to finish the journey on the march, heading towards Ypres in the dust and heat from a hard Belgian road.

I thought how similar the dust from roadworks was to my world of two years earlier, but how different everything else was.

Chapter 6

Enlisting, 1915–1916

During most of 1915, I had been employed on a Public Works job at Raetihi along with my eldest brother, Alf. In September, a group of us were asked to go to Featherston and help in the building of an army training camp to be based there. For the first three weeks, Alf was not well. I persuaded him to return with me to Raetihi.

After about 10 days, I became very discontented with the job. I felt very alone. Nearly all my mates from the Works job had already enlisted or were still at Featherston, and Mum and my girlfriend, Ina, were in Palmerston North.

I decided to go into Raetihi township and enlist. I went from 17 to 20 in two strokes of ink. It was easy to give a false date of birth. I was known from the Public Works job and no one had had reason to question my age before. As I was mainly known by my first name, I hoped the enlisting officer would have no reason to question my surname either. I changed that from Coley to Collins. I still wasn't satisfied that I would be allowed to enlist if the truth was found out. I naturally gave my next of kin as my father, but because that would have kept me a Coley, I turned my dad into my uncle. I now had a new age, a new surname and a new parent.

I had to wait until the first week in December before I was notified that I was accepted as a recruit. I kept wondering if someone would discover my real age and name and that I'd get imprisoned before even leaving New Zealand. It didn't happen. But when I realised there could be implications in what I had done, I knew I had to tell my family before I left. They were none too pleased when I said that if they got mail for a Private Leonard Collins that he was me. We only argued about it that once.

I was sent a train pass and told that I would have to proceed to Trentham Camp on the 15th of December. On the night of the 14th, 22 of us were given a civic farewell in the town hall at Ohakune. It was called a dance. It was more like a smoke concert, card party and shickeroo. I hadn't yet touched alcohol and although I had plenty of it offered to me, again I avoided it that night. Consequently, I was the only one who was sober when the 22 of us arrived at 9am to catch the train to Wellington.

The station was crowded, beflagged and decorated. Nearly all of Ohakune were present to see us join the special troop train that had started from Auckland, collecting enlisted men along the way. Everyone on the platform that morning was animated. No one would have believed Ohakune was in the middle of a dry area. There was beer by the bottle and the barrel with the womenfolk acting as barmaids to all and sundry. The train waited for half an hour while those already on it had breakfast. The rest of us were caught up in the shouting and cheering, and kissing from every local woman who wanted to hug us goodbye.

We arrived at Wellington station by evening, and marched through the town to the Buckle Street Barracks, being given a very warm welcome from bystanders. It seemed to take as long marching through the streets as it had sitting on the train. We slept at the barracks and, next morning, we were marched all the way back to the station to catch the train to Trentham.

Within one hour, we had all been medically examined. Within two hours, we had taken the oath to King and country. I said goodbye to liberty.

That afternoon, we were fitted out in army uniforms. The very next morning, we turned out at drill in them. I found it very easy to get caught up in the newness and excitement.

Two days later and we again took the train to a camp at Maymorn, just north of Upper Hutt, where the township of Heretaunga was being formed. I was here for six weeks through Christmas and January as we were put through the first of our training schedules. As soon as Featherston Camp was ready for occupation, although it was not completed, we were transferred there for the next stage of our training. We were given what was called our final leave and instructed to return to Featherston when our leave expired. We were told that if we were an hour late, we would be arrested.

Halfway through my leave, which I spent in and around Palmerston North seeing Mum and Ina, I became sick with a fever. The local military doctor, Doctor Peach, prevented me from returning to camp. He had three other doctors examine me, and although I kept denying it, they all decided I had rheumatics. They extended my leave pass for a few more days, all signing it, saving me from probably being arrested before I had even begun anything.

When I was ready to return to camp, Doctor Peach gave me a bulky envelope to hand in at headquarters. Because I was later than expected, I went by train to Wellington and Trentham Camp where I met up with the other men who had had to march over the Rimutaka Hill from Featherston.

On the train journey my curiosity got the better of me and

I opened the envelope. It was as well that I did. The doctors recommended my discharge. They wrote that they had no doubt that I had had rheumatic fever. It was probably true. I had had a form of muscular rheumatic fever when I turned 16, and had relapsed a few months later to be laid up for the rest of that year.

I stared at the medical papers on my lap. I decided that the worst that could happen to me was to be dumped from the army if anyone actually found out what the doctors had written. I put my leave pass safely into my pocket, and tore the remaining papers into as many little pieces as I could. As the train ran alongside the coast just before Wellington, I threw the lot out the carriage window.

When I arrived at Trentham Camp, the military policeman on duty at the gate told me to report to headquarters next morning. I refused to give him my pass and trusted to luck that I could find a way to satisfactorily explain my lateness. I was only asked a few questions, there was no threat of punishment for lateness and it was the last I ever heard about the incident.

Unfortunately, there was a blow to come. The men were to sail in three days and because I had not completed my final musketry and shooting courses, I was to be transferred to the 12th Reinforcement. They would not be sailing for another month. I pleaded that I had proved myself the third best shot in the company. I pleaded in vain. I found it very hard to part from my mates at this late stage. I thought them a hard-looking crew of men but I liked them all.

I wasn't beaten. When the men embarked three days later, I was there, waiting with my kit-bag. I tried to sneak aboard. I was seen and stopped. I had to answer a lot of questions but none of my answers was accepted. A red cap was given the responsibility to see that I did not get aboard. I couldn't persuade him to look the other way.

The red cap gave me every opportunity to shout goodbye to my mates but I was not given a chance to make another attempt to get aboard. I surprised myself with tears in my eyes when the boat finally left the wharf.

The next day, I was drafted to J Company, the 12th. They were a good crowd but I never really settled down while I was with them. My heart was with the boys of B11. J Company was made up of mounteds transferred to the infantry. Word had been received that no more mounteds were wanted. Apparently, there were too many already in Egypt and the demand for them had changed. They had been useless on the Gallipoli Peninsula and the peninsula was now being abandoned anyway.

I had an easy time with J Company. I already knew the drill and only had to complete my two final musketry courses. Because of this, I was attached to the buglers. But I had one piece of immense satisfaction from my time with J Company.

I turned out to be the crack shot of them all. From being left behind by B11 and from being the youngest in J12, I got status from this recognition.

In May 1916, we eventually sailed on the *Mokoia*, accompanied by the *Navua*, a slow and lame duck of a troop carrier in the tremendous seas that continually came aboard on the crossing to Australia.

After stopping at Albany in Western Australia, we reached Colombo on the 4th of June, my 18th birthday. We only just made it into the harbour. As we rounded the heads, the *Mokoia* described a large half-circle with the port of Colombo on the starboard bow. All of us rushed to the starboard side, craning our necks for a better view, when the ship suddenly listed dangerously. We all rushed for the port side to try and redistribute the weight. The ship righted only after giving us a jolly good scare. The skipper, Captain Thompson, was not happy with us but as a Christian man, he used Christian language. Our colonel was not so polite.

We dropped anchor in mid-stream and waited. Local boys dived around the ship for coins, ignoring the copper and looking only for silver. We were told that there would be no shore leave for anyone. Apparently our cousins, the Aussies, had left a few days earlier for Egypt. Some of them had been cheated when changing money with local natives. In reprisal, the Aussies wisely bypassed the native quarters but looted shops in the European quarter creating a lot of damage.

Colombo glistened at us like a huge emerald in the sunshine. The picture was enticing. We cursed those Aussies. The penalty we received because of them was a nasty pill to swallow.

For three days, our ship took coal aboard. The dust was suffocating. No amount of fruit from the dozens of local boats that came out to see us could make up for being grilled by the sun and choked by coal dust while the ship was loaded at a pace that was primitively slow.

On the last day in Colombo, we were taken ashore in barges to spend a few hours in the barracks that had been converted into a bazaar for our benefit. It was certainly a pleasant break from coaling — but it was temporary. When we returned on board, we had once more to face the dust during the final loading.

An hour out from Colombo, we picked up our escort of one destroyer. It accompanied us for the next week until we entered the Red Sea and began our preparations for landing at Suez.

As we entered the port, dozens of Gyppos rowed out in small boats, catamarans sailing among them, to greet us.

Their noise was deafening. They continually cut across the bows of our boat causing our captain to pull frequent blasts on the ship's whistle. This only made the din worse.

We had hardly tied up when the locals swarmed aboard. They dragged baskets of fruit, chocolates and cigarettes with them. They fought one another in their frantic haste to do business with us. It was more hectic than in Colombo. And the fruit we had taken aboard at Colombo had gone bad and been dumped at sea. I was desperate for fruit to counteract the heavy food on board that had left me feeling washed out for every couple hours after eating.

Everything was cheap, the locals changed our money themselves, and business became fast and furious. Cigarettes were so cheap that nearly all of us, even those of us who didn't smoke, bought a tin of 50 for 5 piastres, about a shilling. I tried one. I managed half of it before I was leaning over the rail trying to forget the world. It was made worse by the hordes of flies that swooped into my mouth, ears and nose. With one hand I held the rail, and as I retched my other hand tried to swat flies from my face. They would not be driven away and dodged the danger of my flailing arm to attack me again. When I did kill one, another dozen came to the funeral. The locals took no notice of the flies and their faces were a living mass of them. I eventually gave up, accepted the torture and concentrated on being sick from the cigarette.

Most of my mates were suddenly throwing their cigarettes into the water in disgust. When we had nearly all been sick, we went through the usual red tape and formalities and disembarked straight on to the waiting train. In the five-minute wait before the train left the port, we solved the puzzle of the cigarettes turning us up. As soon as anyone threw away a cigarette, a Gyppo pounced on it. He broke away the charred end of tobacco, removed the remaining paper and put the tobacco into a small bag that he carried. When he had a few ounces, he sold it to another Gyppo who was the cigarette maker. This was mixed with a grade of cheap tobacco and made into a fresh cigarette. As soon as we all realised this, it became a rare sight to see anyone throw away a butt. Instead, the butt was crushed into the sand and destroyed. (Months later in France, I saw how difficult it was for men to get out of this habit.)

The two-hour train journey from Suez was through terrific dry heat and sand. Visits to the wet canteen for iced beer helped us sweat in relief. Our destination camp was at Tel-el-Kebir, near the site of the old battlefield of the same name. On one side of the canal, which was lined with date palms, were the station, a few shops and houses, and numerous open-air bazaars. On the other side were crops of rice, grapes, watermelons and oranges. The orange grove made a fine sight and my mouth watered. A steel bridge about 2 chains long spanned the canal and gave access to our camp that was sited between the camps for the Aussies and the Tommies. Except for a couple of wooden buildings, the whole show was under canvas.

When detailed to our tents, I had the idea that we were meant to either roast at night with 10 of us in each bell tent or get very lousy. Two of us decided to sleep in the open in preference to pigging it in the tent. I went to sleep under a veil of stars.

About two in the morning, I woke up shivering. My blankets and uniform were wet through as if I had been dumped in a bath. At first I thought it was rain but the sky was still covered in stars. I discovered the hard way that desert dew and desert cold swept everywhere in the few hours before sunrise. Within minutes of the sun rising, the heat of the day was back in full force. It was not surprising that I got a dose of sand colic from swallowing too much sand my first morning. It left me pretty crook for a whole week.

Our daily routine had us up at 3.30am, coffee, on parade by 4am, and finished with drill for the day at 5am because of the rising heat. We had the occasional night manoeuvres but it was often so dark after sunset that I found it easy to leave the parade and fall in again when the men returned so that I was present at roll call.

Regular roll calls were necessary. It was easy to go astray. Many of us went souvenir hunting to the battlefield of Tel-el-Kebir about 1½ miles away. But to go singly was forbidden. To go out of camp without our water bottle and enough food in the form of biscuits for one good meal was likewise forbidden.

Once in the open desert it was easy to be fooled by distances and mirages. And not long after our arrival here, two of our men did get lost, one of them dying from thirst and sunburn. Three days after he was reported missing, he was found having discarded his clothes, probably in his eagerness to reach some imagined water. His naked body was an awful sight after being cooked by the sun.

It didn't take long in a camp such as this for the men to start taking a rise out of the locals because of their ignorance of English. If any of us repeated the headlines of the paper in front of the newspaper boys, they would yell the headlines at everyone else, but blissfully unaware of what they were shouting. And our wags played on it.

On the day news came through that Lord Kitchener had drowned when HMS *Hampshire* struck a mine,* I was startled to hear the paper boys yelling 'Good news this

---

* Field Marshal Lord Kitchener was a career soldier who served in many conflicts, including the 1899–1902 South African War, before becoming Secretary for War in August 1914. He had visited New Zealand in 1910 to advise on the organisation of the armed forces. HMS *Hampshire* was mined off Orkney on 5 June 1916.

morning, Kitchener drowned, good news this morning.' When someone wanted to put one across the camp adjutant, Captain Glover, a rather pompous man, we were woken with the paper boys yelling 'Good news this morning, Captain Glover steals the colonel's wife.'

The poor boys were chased by an irate captain brandishing his cane. The next morning, the sensational news was reversed. 'Good news, colonel steals captain's wife.' This was followed by another chase. It wasn't long before every morning had its various joke, sometimes ingenious, sometimes a malicious dig at someone not in popular favour with the originator.

The local Gyppos were not allowed inside any of the camps without a special pass. If any were caught breaking these rules, their gendarmes were terribly severe on them. One morning at breakfast, one of our men persuaded a local boy of about 15 to come into the lines for some spare bread. A gendarme spotted the boy and grabbed him. We made him let the boy go and the boy wandered off in the sand to eat the bread. Suddenly, we heard several yells. The gendarme was beating the boy with his cane. As some of us rushed over, the gendarme bolted.

The boy's face was an awful mess and his nose was clearly broken. Our doctor plastered him up and sent him home. I mightn't have thought any more about the incident except for what happened that night.

Working gangs of locals came and went every four hours of the day and always entered the camps from the bridge by the station. Two Gyppo gendarmes, armed with canes and short swords, and two of our military police, were always on duty on the bridge at sunset when the area was packed with crowds flocking around the bazaars. The working gangs would always sing their droning dirges whether going to or coming from work, giving the impression that they were surprisingly happy. This night, a gang crossed the bridge chanting merrily as usual. Before anyone had time to realise what took place, the gang closed on one of the gendarmes and literally cut him to pieces with his own sword. Many of the gang leapt into the canal and swam to safety. No one attempted to stop them. It soon became known that the murdered gendarme was the one who had beaten the boy so badly earlier in the day. I had witnessed local justice.

That incident had me wonder about the way some of our own men treated the locals. Because the Gyppos overloaded and overpriced everything, some of our men did their best to undermine them. We would try and cheat them of beer from an overladen wagon, pulled by a single donkey, that had become stuck in the sand. We would bargain them out of watermelons, sometimes upending their cart to grab melons before they could save them. We would torment the kids by grabbing oranges, dates or figs when a mate diverted their attention. And we would act innocently in front of our officers called by the Gyppos to help. Most of the time with the kids it was mischief and we gave them back their goods when we tired of teasing, or even paid the kids more than they had originally asked.

What I didn't eat were grapes. I was put off by watching what they used to wash and shine each grape.

While I was on camp picket one morning with Tommy Spearman and Fred McFarlane, both boxing champs from Wellington, I came as near to being killed as at any other time that was to come during the next years of the war. For something to do to ease the boredom, we began teasing a boy of about 16 over his fruit. Suddenly, he whipped out an open clasp knife and lunged at me. As I tried to sidestep him, his knife cut my equipment belt. Fred planted his boot into the boy's stomach and he dropped the knife, gasping for breath. Tommy jumped on him and held him. I recovered from my surprise and grabbed the knife. I told Tommy to let him go. I gave the boy his knife back. Fred and Tommy stared in surprise before telling me I was an idiot. But I was ready for him if he tried anything. I simply wanted to try out something I had read once.

The change in the boy was remarkable. He closed the knife, put it away and literally fell all over me. From that moment on, Ahmed became a willing slave to me. When I looked out of the tent in the morning, he was there, waiting. Wherever I went, he followed 2 yards behind. He carried my washing and drinking water, polished my boots and buttons, and bought almost everything I wanted at less cost than I could have. Ahmed appointed himself my bodyguard, guide, and instructor in the Egyptian language.

Early in this relationship, I thought of him as a damned nuisance and once tried to give him the slip. When he found me, he was so hurt and dejected that I couldn't again steel my heart to such an action. I actually became very fond of him. Of course, the men chiacked me like mad for a few days, but I took no notice when I realised Ahmed would not so much as raise a finger to do a single thing for any of my mates. He thus became both a treasure and a nuisance.

I became fascinated by the bargains in good quality silk. Locals made souvenir cushions and cards or scarves while we waited. The work was done by machine and I was amazed at the cleverness with which they worked the most difficult designs and never hesitated over them. I simply selected the silk and design, and in 15 or 20 minutes the finished article was ready for posting to my mum and Ina.

I often stopped to watch the evening entertainment from other locals, such as the circus or fakirs. That is, if a couple of donkeys, three or four mangy camels, two horses and a few snarling mongrel dogs could be called a circus. But Ben Ali, the magician, was a great favourite. His tricks were wonderful and the whole desert was his stage. His only apparatus was his clothing under which he must have carried everything. Yet try as I did, I never saw his hands come into contact with his clothes. With his monotonously repetitive incantation of 'gulli, gulli, gulli', he would produce eggs or chickens or snakes from out of nowhere.

Because the daytime heat was always about 115° F, cards, crown and anchor and two-up were the only recreations. I don't include beer drinking. That was a solemn rite for those who indulged in it. I was yet to learn its importance. I preferred to develop what there was to develop in the art of two-up.

And it was here in Egypt that I met the army biscuit, which I could not develop any kind of taste for. To eat one, it had to be broken into small pieces and soaked first in tea. The biscuit was as hard as the hobs of the place parsons talk about. Only the farriers collected them, but not for themselves. The mules in camp had to be kept shod. But the mules strongly objected. It often took four men all day to shoe two mules, if they hadn't strangled them in frustration first. A farrier had thrown some army biscuits at a mule telling it to go choke itself. He discovered that the mule loved the biscuits and tormented him for more. He saw the possibilities and rounded up biscuits from the tents. It became the easiest of tasks for the farriers to slap a dozen shoes on the mules while they crunched away.

The medical staff filled in their days by regularly giving me castor oil for the sand colic. They further justified their position with inoculation orgies. I was in Egypt for seven and a half weeks and inoculated six times. Their excuse was malaria, tetanus, smallpox — and goodness knows what the other ones were for unless they were to guard against dying from a natural death.

During these weeks, and after I had recovered from the colic, I was given five days' leave to go to Cairo. As soon as I stepped on to the railway platform, I was faced with a selection of jostling, squabbling and swearing boys, all waving written references in English at me, all claiming a background as the best and most honest guide in the whole of Cairo.

They were, as Ahmed was, so serious and eager to see that I stayed in safe hands, theirs, that I couldn't get annoyed with them. I read some of the references. Oh, dear, some of my army mates obviously thought themselves wags. What some poor kid fancied was a splendid reference to his sterling qualities was generally nothing more than an indictment of his family history or of his ability as the worst swindler born. Some were actually funny and signed by 'George, RJ, the King' or 'Julius Caesar' or 'Prince of Whales'. Some were horribly low as a trick to have played and I tore one up saying, 'No good, no good'. I was understood.

My first stop was at the Anzac Club, half a mile from the station. I wanted to begin with a clean meal. And I immediately met another round of young boys. As I and others ate, I could feel my boots being cleaned beneath the table. As they were finished, a chubby little black face appeared above the edge of the table followed by a grubby little hand held out for payment. The face disappeared and began on the next man's dusty boots.

I realised that I was quite fond of the local children. They all seemed to know the value of their small personalities, baby-like charm and innocent appeal. About the age of 16, they changed suddenly. They became sly and eager to take us down at the slightest chance. All I wanted to do was use my boot on them.

I spent hours at the museum, the Blue Mosque, a school, the well that Joseph was supposed to have been lowered into by his brethren and the Citadel Mosque that was built as a half-size replica of the Taj Mahal. I was overwhelmed with the white marble and beauty of stately columns and wonderful altars. It appealed to my eyes and imagination, but I was aware it left my heart unstirred. As I watched worshippers prostrate themselves on beautiful rugs, I kept hearing the words from a hymn, 'the heathen in his blindness bows down to wood and stone'. But these were words of white missionaries and Christ who also said 'love your enemies'. So what was I doing in Egypt? Was I here to love my enemies? These words and thoughts irritated me and I couldn't clear them from my mind.

Our padre, who seemed to know Egypt as he knew human nature, had given us all a piece of advice when we arrived at camp.

He said, 'Boys, while you're in Egypt, you will see life in its raw state, its sordid, filthy state. You will think it strange when I say this, but I want you all to see it. Look for it and do not go away from Egypt until you have seen these things. If you will do this, I will feel that I have done you all the greatest service in my power. Don't forget, look for the evil first, the good will take care of itself. God bless you.'

Coming from such a man, this seemed staggering advice. Naturally, many of us had discussed what he might have meant. My wildest imaginings probably fell far short of any reality. But on the night of my first day sightseeing in Cairo, I recalled the padre's words that had clung to me like a leech. I guessed there was an excellent reason behind them. I decided to go in search of the padre's evil things.

With a mate, Jack, we found a guide. The very first thing the guide said was, 'Ah, so you want to go down to the wazirs. I take you.' On the way, the guide asked, 'Which one? French, English, Spanish, Indian, Egyptian . . .?' I realised that every nationality was represented in their houses of ill-fame. For some reason, I chose a French one. Jack nodded as if that suited him too.

The guide spoke to a huge Nubian outside a door. The Nubian turned to me and asked if I wished to see any specialities. I speak nothing but the truth when I say I was innocent of women and the ways of wazirs. I therefore had absolutely no idea what my answer meant when I said, 'Yes, specialities.' The big Nubian showed no surprise at my answer and beckoned Jack and me to follow.

We were led into a large room in the middle of which was a peculiar kind of upholstered table about 18 inches high. It was padded like a divan or mattress. We were told to sit in chairs that were some distance from the table. My feelings were getting so mixed that I didn't know what was happening inside me. I do know that I wanted to bolt from the place but forced myself to stay in the chair. I heard the door lock behind us. The Nubian disappeared behind some curtains but quickly returned, telling us we would have to wait a few minutes until they were ready.

A small bell tinkled somewhere behind the curtains, the Nubian clapped his hands twice, the curtains parted and eight girls filed into the room. They were absolutely naked except for a flimsy loin-cloth each wore. Even that was not necessary, for it hid nothing. I went all shades of all colours. I still wanted to run but looked at the Nubian. He smiled and fingered the wicked-looking knife strapped around his waist. I was totally unarmed. I accepted the inevitable.

By this time, the girls, most of whom were very attractive,

were performing a dance akin to the cancan. But it was without skirts and pants. When the dance finished, Jack and I were invited to choose a girl by pointing to her. Jack and I looked at each other, neither of us attempting to point anywhere. The Nubian spoke two names and dismissed the rest.

I hadn't paid any fee yet and tried to suggest to the Nubian that we pay half and go. He clearly didn't want half. He wanted the lot — but he wasn't going to accept the full amount until everything had been gone through. Even together, Jack and I were not in a position to argue with this huge man.

I had no say in what followed, as the armed Nubian at the doorway was an effective bar to any rash thought on my part, but the dance seemed mild in comparison. I hadn't believed that any young woman, and a fine-looking one at that to make things worse, could lend herself to such staggering acts. I knew only too well that I couldn't bluff myself that I was in the middle of a terrible nightmare.

I gladly paid and rushed outside. It was my first experience of actually being with a woman. I stood in the street, shame, horror, mortification and even rage struggling for mastery over me.

I left Jack and walked the main street of the city all that night on my own. Bed was impossible. It was obvious that I had gone to a wazir, it was obvious what would happen when I was there, yet I was horrified with myself for having done the obvious when it was also obvious that I had had a choice. As I wandered again through the Blue Mosque, I began to understand the padre.

Over the next two days, I travelled out to Luxor and back to see history and settle myself. As I began to leave the station, haggling with several guides, two young Englishwomen pulled up in their private car and offered to show me around for an hour, or more if I fancied. They were so charming that I couldn't refuse. After a meal, one left and, as the other said she was a good piano player, I readily agreed to go to her apartment for some music. And could she play. I lay back on her divan, contented. Suddenly she was beside me. I was embarrassed but liked her nearness. I kissed her. I went red and she teased me. Laughingly, she said anything else would cost me 150 piastres.

I was too stunned to speak. My mind pictured the French girls in the wazir, like caged humans. I heard the word 'syphilis' being tersely hissed at me from one of the guides. I had thought what a kind and gracious woman this piano player was and how different her place was from the wazir. Yet she had picked me up solely for money, and I hadn't realised it. Again, I felt disgust and repulsion surge through me. In two minutes I was standing in the street, loathing all women. Why, I asked myself, must I run into this kind of woman?

All I had looked for was some goodness. It suddenly seemed that all the dreams and ideals that had been part of my early training and tuition, and all the ideals my mother had striven to instill in me, had been shattered. I understood the padre even more. I thanked him from where I was on the street. But as I walked back to the Anzac Club, I found it hard to see any woman as decent. I was fast tarring them all with the same brush. I did realise the injustice of such an opinion and tried to rid myself of it, but I finished the day at the club, without the heart to go anywhere and feeling too mortified and too shamed.

I visited Cairo again as its fascination never ceased to grip me. But for all its antiquity, glory and gorgeousness of scenes and sights, and depravity of its slums, I felt it impossible to have a picture of Cairo without the sordid, rampant and predominating human feature of sex.

Little did I dream then that in the next three years the grim starkness of war would teach me to treat such things as inevitable.

We prepared to move from our camp. Those of us in J Company were given the choice of joining the Camel Corps or going to France. We were told that we would not get horses at any time, so it was camels or the infantry. About six chose camels. I had seen enough of them to do me.

Rations were issued and we embarked late at night by train for Alexandria. The journey took all night and we were in open wagons in the bitter cold. Most of us were wet to our skins with the heavy dew that fell like light rain. But by 7.30am, after the sun had been up for a few hours, we were dry and on the wharf waiting to board the *Ivernia*. (She was torpedoed about 15 months later in mid-ocean.)

Everything was clean and comfortable with plenty of room for the 2000 of us, including 500 from a Tommy battalion. The harbour entrance was about a mile away and was liberally sown with both floating and submerged mines. A channel ran down the centre but on an angle so that the mines overlapped. It took us two hours to get through. It was not a healthy spot for the steering gear to fail.

We were greeted by an escort of two destroyers to keep an eye on the sea around us. No risks were to be taken. There were lookouts in the rigging of the *Ivernia* during daylight, 20 men were on guard on each side of the ship day and night, smoking was absolutely forbidden on deck between dusk and daylight, portholes were painted black, every bulkhead door was manned continually. Boat drill was held twice each day and once each night to make sure there would be no mistakes if we were hit.

The trip took seven days and was only just uneventful. As we entered Marseilles heads, a French boat with about 500 reservists aboard passed heading out to the open sea. We were not a mile apart when I heard a terrific explosion. A huge column of water descended onto the French troopship. Within minutes, six destroyers tore past at full speed.

As we berthed, two returned with survivors and news of about 50 casualties.

Almost in contradiction of this news, we were given a wonderful welcome. Wine and bread, fruit, tea and cakes and confectionery were simply showered on us. Souvenir cards and miniature tricolours made up their gifts. Some of us gave what souvenirs we could and our band played a couple of tunes. In a few hours we had transferred from ship to train and, as we steamed slowly away from Marseilles for an unknown destination, a local band followed playing 'La Marseillaise', everyone singing, whistling and yelling to the strains of the music. I had never realised before how stirring music could be. Everyone was at a fever pitch of excitement.

Our first major stop was at Lyons. As we pulled into the station, I could see dozens of trestle tables laid out in snowy linen and covered in glasses. Another dense crowd welcomed us. I was overwhelmed with smiling mesdames and mesdemoiselles and old gentlemen kissing me on both cheeks and passing on to the next man to treat him the same.

My mate, Arthur Hall, yelled to me, 'Stand your ground, Len. Let them come to you.' It was good advice. I got several doses of kisses that way.

Our dinner was the greatest feast I think I ever saw. There was so much food and wine, and champagne flowed like water. It was fun trying to both understand and make myself understood by the locals. My French–English guide was worth its weight in gold.

'Mon brave soldat' came from the lips of every French person who spoke to me. And I had yet to fire or hear a shot.

The hospitality shown to us was magnificent and, in those few hours, the people of Lyons endeared themselves to us for all time. It warmed me and I felt love for them. I might forget other places in life, but never Lyons.

We were all too soon rolling through mile after mile of vineyards. It was the loveliest country I could wish to set eyes on. I thought that it was no wonder that France was trying to save itself. It seemed worth fighting for, and perhaps dying for. I was to discover in time that the north of France is totally different with regards to the friendliness of its people. It was like comparing people in New Zealand. Those from the North Island are not a patch on those from the South Island.

Unfortunately, we bypassed Paris and arrived at Calais 52 hours after leaving Marseilles. I tried to pull my boots on but couldn't. My feet had become badly swollen and I couldn't even stand. My legs wouldn't hold me. I was carried to an ambulance and dispatched to an evacuation hospital on the wharf.

As the submarines were apparently having a merry time in the English Channel, we were going to be held up for two days before crossing to England for special camp. None of us had done any significant training in the two months since reaching Egypt and we had to be brought up to the mark.

Half of the staff of the wharf hospital was French and the other half English. I had to stay in bed but there was no sign of any ache in me anywhere. The doctors said it was probably rheumatics. When they asked if I had ever had that before, I stoutly lied. If I had said 'yes', it would have been all over for me. To get this far and then get fired strahome again did not appeal one little bit.

I saw nothing of the city as my mates did but I continually watched the activity on the wharf. In those two days, the only ships entering or leaving the port were hospital carriers. Departures for England with the wounded and sick averaged one ship per hour. All of them were full.

The swelling in my feet went down and I rejoined my mates. We sailed for England to head to Sling Camp near Bulford on the Salisbury Plains among villages with scenes of wooded hillsides, old mills, rustic bridges and streams choked with fresh watercress. From almost anywhere, I could see the spire of Salisbury Cathedral piercing the sky.

Within a few weeks, laden with equipment and ready to fight, we were back on the train to northern France and the region known as the Somme. We were a new division, including many veterans from Gallipoli and Egypt. We were all, though, untried in the trench warfare of the Western Front. And even as a crack shot in training, I was untried in killing.

Chapter 7

Ypres and Passchendaele, 1930

I am numbed by today. I have stood at two memorials for dead and missing men. I was told of 100,000 soldiers lost in the ground forever around Ypres and Passchendaele. Some I knew. I have difficulty picturing them. Yet 100,000 is not anything like the real number. So many disappeared into the mud, drowned and interred. They didn't stand a chance. Some didn't even fire a shot. That's a hard thought to accept. A young man enlists in New Zealand, trains for months to handle his gun and himself and be part of a team, steps into no man's land for the very first time at Ypres, and dies, drowned in mud or ripped to pieces on barbed wire.

Ypres. The very name is graven on the mind of the whole empire — perhaps the world. Memories crowd my mind by the mere mention of the name. Ypres. Stories under its name suggest deeds of valour and superhuman struggles for victory. The troops called it 'Wipers'. Our stories tell tales of horrible, sudden death and depict scenes of fearful agonies, ruin and desolation, mud and misery. It brings a living death to my mind.

The Cloth Hall is being rebuilt. Belgium is trying to duplicate what had been an architectural offering to the world. I am told it could take 30 years or more.

The Menin Gate Memorial at Ypres was opened on the 24th July, 1927. Three years later, names are still being carved on it. I am told that could take another 10 years.

Menin Gate and Tyne Cot Cemetery, not far away at Passchendaele, could never give enough recognition to what took place here. How does anyone? It was barbaric slaughter — for both sides. Many headstones say nothing more than 'Known unto God'. And outside Menin Gate, 8 o'clock at night, every night, all traffic stops. Locals, men of the Ypres Fire Brigade, play the Last Post over the thousands of bodies never found.

I watch a farmer plough a field. He has found fertile land and makes furrows across its brow. I wonder what's hidden behind the frown. I heard a story of another farmer being blown to pieces just a few months ago when he ploughed into an unexploded bomb. Apparently it's happened several times. I heard stories of other farmers unearthing bones.

The farmer I watch is industrious. He looks as if he belongs. I hope he does. He's planted trees along the edges of his field. They're bigger than I am. When I left, there wasn't one, not one for as far as I could see, not even a twig sticking up from the mud. Some areas of pre-war forest have started to grow as if a memorial to themselves.

The earth needs healing too. I can smell burnt flesh of men and mules. I lift a lump from a furrow and expect it to release an arm or a leg or even a cloud of gas. It doesn't. But I splutter anyway.

As I walk on, cornfields wave, and closer to the village there are pretty and attended gardens. The estaminets are noisy, adults laugh inside them, and on the streets children argue in play. The locals have returned and the villages are being rebuilt. They've had just 12 years. But they say they've already heard the rumblings once again across the border.

As far back as 1922, someone called Adolf Hitler vowed 'vengeance' for the two million fallen Germans of the Great War. If that were true and I lived here, I could lose my sanity. Since the war, I have often felt nothing more than a corpse floating in a shell hole of stagnant water poisoned from gas. And I haven't been ploughing fields of shell holes.

Last night, some of the men recalled songs from the trenches. 'If you were the only girl in the world . . .', 'Pack up your troubles in your old kit bag . . .', and 'We're here because we're here because we're here because we're here . . .'

Our voices trailed off. Tears dried up inside. We probably lost ourselves in memories of nightmares. It crossed my mind that I was here now because I was here then.

Some of us pulled out extracts of war poems penned by soldiers like us. I had some of Siegfried Sassoon's, the British officer who had received the Military Cross at the Somme in 1916. A year later, Sassoon had thrown his MC into the Mersey in protest at the continuation of the war.

I read from his short 'Memorial Tablet', written just as the war ended in 1918. *I died in hell.* His haunting words from Passchendaele about the soldier struggling to safety when a shell explodes on the duckboards — *so I fell / Into the bottomless mud, and lost the light…*

Another read from Sassoon's 'Aftermath', written in 1919 when he already had reasons to challenge us all . . . *Have you forgotten yet? Look up and swear by the green of the spring that you'll never forget.*

I can't picture all those bodies. I can't picture how many hundred thousand pieces there would be. There was nothing to savour from my months at Ypres. It was unsurpassed horror. I contributed to it. I can't even think of the number of young German men I would have killed. They are here too, beneath my boots.

Chapter 8

Passchendaele, 1917

The last part of the journey to Ypres might have been a short march, and it might have been autumn, 29th September, but we arrived under another blistering sun, covered with dust. My shoulders were chafed raw from the drag of my heavy equipment. My clothing stuck to me, and body lice — from God knows where, given all my washing and swimming — were back tormenting me. I was sick of marching mile after mile on cobblestones. I felt like falling from sheer fatigue and needed more water.

Our dugouts were in the sheltered side of the Yser Canal Bank, about a quarter of a mile from the famous Cloth Hall on the other side of a huge, cobblestone square. But at that hour of the afternoon not all the cloth halls in the world would have interested me. I washed and bathed my feet.

Some Scottish troops were billeted close by and, as soon as I was settling down for rest, they came over for a yarn. All of us New Zealanders were fond of the Jocks and made them as welcome as possible. Our arrival had apparently caused alarm. The first questions from the Jocks were about their concerns.

'Have you boys been out training?'

<u>Armentières</u>. <u>Description</u>. <u>Before</u> and after the <u>Somme</u>.

On the morning of October 12th, 1916, the 2nd Brigade N.Z.E.F, returned to Armentières from the Somme. It was a beautiful morning, with just a faint chill of early Winter in the air. This was the first many of us had seen of the beautiful old town, and it gave us a sense of peace, it looked so venerable. Entering The Square, one received a shock. The only building damaged was the Cathedral, and it had been attended to in a very thorough manner by the German gunners. The roof was completely shattered, while great jagged holes appeared in the walls. On entering, the Altar caught your attention immediately. It was intact, and all fallen debris had been cleared away by the French people,[†] for a distance of 20 ft all around it, and they still continued to use it for their Services, which were held as ~~usual~~, in pre war days., ~~Though only about 30 French people remained in the city, they never tired~~ of doing all ~~they could for us, and that was~~ a large order. the worshippers being called to prayer by the ringing of a small hand bell, but this we learned later. ~~Those~~ of our men who could get away, often joined them, and the French people loved them for it, though I never saw more than 10 of our boys there at any one time. Turning to go out again, one noticed what had once been a beautiful big stained glass window, but there was something which made you study what was left of it. There was a figure,

Mealtime — serving up at the field kitchen.
Kippenberger Military Archive, Army Museum Waiouru, H-501

Members of the New Zealand Rifles Brigade near the line at Ypres.
Kippenberger Military Archive, Army Museum Waiouru, H-251

Cheering on a wounded soldier.
KIPPENBERGER MILITARY ARCHIVE, ARMY MUSEUM WAIOURU, H-432

The advanced dressing station, Battle of Messines Ridge.
KIPPENBERGER MILITARY ARCHIVE, ARMY MUSEUM WAIOURU, H-62

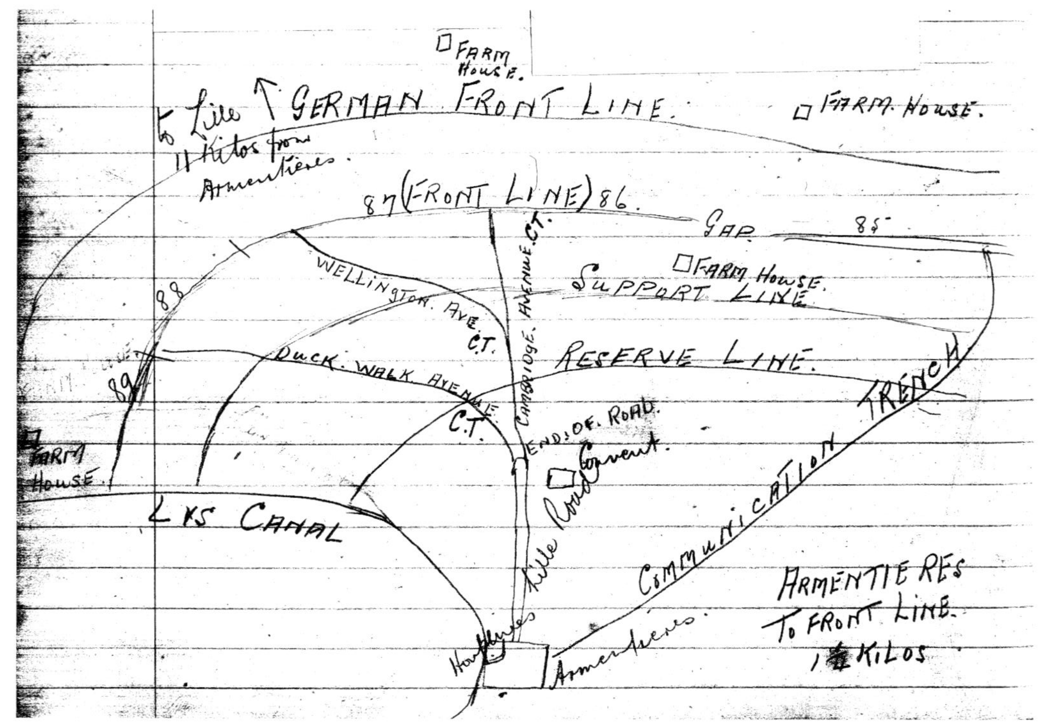

Trench arrangements near Armentières, as sketched by Len Coley.
PROPERTY OF THE AUTHOR

An observation post.
KIPPENBERGER MILITARY ARCHIVE, ARMY MUSEUM WAIOURU, H-424

Mealtime in the trench, Somme.
KIPPENBERGER MILITARY ARCHIVE, ARMY MUSEUM WAIOURU, H-468

Helping French civilians.
KIPPENBERGER MILITARY ARCHIVE, ARMY MUSEUM WAIOURU, H-507

New Zealanders outside a dressing station.
KIPPENBERGER MILITARY ARCHIVE, ARMY MUSEUM WAIOURU, H-182

Len and Ivy's wedding day, 1937.
MARRIOTT FAMILY COLLECTION

Len and Ivy, circa 1937.
MARRIOTT FAMILY COLLECTION

Len Coley, left, standing behind his nephew, the author, Allan Marriott, in 1953.
MARRIOTT FAMILY COLLECTION

Len thanked the support of the Salvation Army padres during the First World War by later assisting as a volunteer.
MARRIOTT FAMILY COLLECTION

Len Coley in 1960, Masterton.

'Are you here for a stunt?'

'Some Aussies are already here, are the rest following you boys?'

'When does the stunt come off?'

We answered truthfully, 'yes, yes, yes,' but as to when, we knew as much or as little as they did. One big fellow expressed what seemed to be a general opinion among the Jocks.

'We knew there must be something on when all you colonials started to arrive.'

One of our men called back, 'Never mind, Jock, let's hope you boys are on one of our flanks, then we can feel safe.'

This approach pleased them immensely. I liked the idea of going into a big stunt side by side with them. The Jocks had a reputation for being splendid fighters. They were sturdy and possessed initiative and self-reliance. This was different from most of the Tommies I had fought alongside. The Tommies were too often born and bred to look up to their boss as a 'tin god', and to rely on their immediate superiors. They often lacked the ability to act on their own when called upon to do so.

I rested well, followed by a good meal. I now took a look over my surroundings. It was apparent from when we arrived that we were still some distance from the front line. I could hear our heavy guns about a mile away to the north and east.

The Cloth Hall was a shambles. The tower still stood, but looked ready to collapse at any time. It had clearly been a beautiful building, built in the 13th century, and had been regarded as one of the glories of the world. It was now beyond all hope of repair.

The whole place looked grim and gaunt. Many of the scarred walls of houses were all that was standing among a picture of absolute ruin. The station and railway generally was unusable except for several trains from the army light railway still servicing the sector. The roads had been heavily shelled. We were told that in the first two weeks of August about four and a half million shells had been fired by the British troops ahead of us, let alone the number that would have been fired back. Only rough attempts had been made in places to patch the roads.

The whole countryside looked forbidding. It was a sea of mud, caked dry only on the surface, with shattered trees marring the landscape. Beyond, towards the slopes, I could see the scarred ridges of the front line. These belonged to the Germans who had an uninterrupted view of the greater part of us. It looked exactly like what it was, a shell-torn, muddy and dreary waste. It was probably the most uninviting and unhealthy place in the world.

I heard a question asked of a Jock about what it was like out there. His reply was humorously sarcastic.

'Aye mon, it's noot a place for your health. A mon goot keelled up there yesterday.'

We were soon to find out for ourselves. We began preparations for a move to relieve the 59th Division on the 2nd October. They handed over to us with too much pleasure for my liking, and remarked that it was starting to liven up. Our battalion, 2nd Wellington, took over the old German front line. We had plenty of pill-boxes for shelter and, to start with, found the day quiet. A few of us amused ourselves with stupid and foolish tricks, such as putting Mills bombs in kerosene tins or in water-filled shell holes. One bomb exploded something else unexpected in a shell hole. Four of us were nearly blown up. We stopped the games.

Our position was in a slight dip and so we were not troubled with shellfire. Those on either side of us got a sprinkling of shrapnel at intervals.

On the night of 3rd October, we moved forward a short way into a trench that was only a system of connected shell holes. It was open and cold. I now knew that we would be going over the top in the morning.

And as the night became colder, the feeling of depression that often comes in these moments settled on us all. I thought about the unknown of tomorrow and the terror that can become our worst enemy in the march to the battlefield. I thought about other terrors almost as bad, such as when the field is reached and there is waiting all around us for the first blow to be struck. There is a terror in waiting, waiting, waiting for an order to kill — or an order to be killed.

So it was with me that night. I said several silent prayers. I watched my mates as they said theirs. Words of farewell and cheer were penned and handed to the padre at the last minute. I kept my words to myself. For a while, we could forget the mud and misery and dream of New Zealand and our families so far away.

I knew also that later, even if feeling confident, we would all be wondering if we would go under. The job assigned to us did not seem difficult. True, the country itself, Belgium, was strange, it looked and sounded too German, and the surroundings were strange. This made everything we did seem strange. So we, I, would have to be a little more careful, that was all.

Towards dawn, mist came with a terrible cold air. Drizzle set in. All I could do was lie there and endure it. As the sky lightened, cigarettes were lit all along the line to steady nerves and give some comfort. At 6am, word was passed along to stand to. Cigarettes were smoked in earnest. For a non-smoker, I found it fragrant and welcome.

At 6.10am, in what was to be called the Battle of

Broodseinde, the ball opened with our guns. We could not yet make a move from the trench and had to wait until our barrage at the German front line lifted. When we were told to move, it was initially a painful experience. Every joint was frozen. I was awkward, stiff and as cold as ice. Drizzle became light rain.

As we struggled from the trenches, our eagerness to be on the move took over. I forgot my earlier fear. At long last we were doing something. And did we ever.

The Germans, or those that could, fled in front of us. A few immediately surrendered. We quickly passed the German front line. It seemed to be half full of corpses, far more than I expected. I thought their line was being held by a very strong force.

I paused at a wounded prisoner who was sitting in the mud on the edge of a large shell hole. I said, 'You boys are running.'

He understood me. In broken English, he enlightened me. He said we had beaten them by 10 minutes. They were all at final rest, due to attack us at 6.20am.

To say I was pleased that we had got in first would be to underestimate my feelings. But one thing I thought we could bargain on would be stiff resistance before going much further. I was wrong. Our attack had thrown the German plans completely out of gear for the moment. When their barrage struck back, it was at our empty trenches. Slowly, they dropped their range and their shells began to creep closer from behind. It was too scattered to give us any uneasiness.

Our own barrage was wonderful, like a huge curtain of fire. Our guns sounded magnificent, like a rolling drum from the rear. Many of us suddenly felt so much at home in this, that we used our digging-in shovels as walking sticks to help us through the mud that was slithery and 4 to 6 inches deep.

My Lewis gun was not needed as we advanced and it hung over my shoulder by its sling.

Our first objective had been 1000 yards from hop-off. And until we as the support wave passed through the first wave and became the first wave, there had been no resistance whatsoever. The only action now from Fritz consisted of a few bursts from a single machine gun. We took full advantage of cover in the shell holes while two of our men who were out of their sight dashed up behind the pill-box and each threw in a bomb. It immediately caught fire. We waited while the company on our right silenced three other machine guns in a similar manner. The barrage halted for 20 minutes and gave us plenty of opportunity to see how others were faring.

Everything seemed to have gone splendidly. The Aussies, nearly half a mile away, were busy collecting prisoners. There seemed to be more prisoners than Aussies. Perhaps if the Germans had shown fight, our mates would have had their work cut out to gain their objective. And as we waited, a few prisoners began coming through to us along the line.

Our souvenir king, Jim Farr, grabbed the opportunity that seemed made for his special benefit. He collected watches and field-glasses with a speed and thoroughness that was amazing to see. One of the last prisoners in Jim's waiting line almost became his Waterloo. The German was a well-built man aged about 20. Jim collected his gold watch and stopped to admire it. This was too much for Fritz. He grabbed at his watch with one hand and pushed at Jim with the other. Fritz got his watch and Jim fell backwards into a shell hole. Two of our men pushed the German on his way to our rear.

Jim scrambled from the hole and abused his mates for rushing Fritz away.

'What the hell did you do that for?' he asked in a hurt

way. 'That was the best watch I've seen. My reputation will suffer now that I've lost it and been done by a Hun.'

We laughed fit to burst and joked that we wanted to see it happen again just to see the expression on Jim's face as he took his backward dive. We were so busy throwing off at Jim that I don't think many of us fully realised where we were. A whistle brought us up standing. It was time for the next stage.

Our smiles disappeared and we were on the alert. As we moved forward, we took a half-turn to the left, changing our front by about 45 degrees. Gravenstafel Spur and Abraham Heights were now directly in front. There was still no resistance. The rain ceased for a while. There was plenty of ideal cover for German snipers, but they too, seemed to have disappeared. Our final objective was a further mile away.

We were within 300 yards of this when we encountered sudden and stubborn resistance from the area of Kronprinz Farm. Two machine guns opened up at us followed by snipers. The snipers were clearly more dangerous than the guns. Every time a German sniper fired, one of our boys suddenly dropped dead. The snipers were hidden in trees on the farm, just inside the edge of what had once been a grove of trees known as Berlin Wood. We counted seven snipers.

I was given the job of taking them out. As each one was located, I was directed to turn my Lewis gun on him. It took me 10 minutes before there were no more snipers.

Twice while shooting, I had felt a sudden tug on my back. A mate told me that there were two bullet holes in my haversack. I had been shooting from the rim of a shell hole and my gun had given me just enough protection to make the snipers fire high.

While I was dealing with the snipers, two of our bombers, less than 50 yards away, unloaded on top of the Germans inside Kronprinz Farm. Corporal Neilson called on those inside to surrender. The reply was two bullets, both missing him. Neilson and his men threw bombs inside. When it was safe to do so, they rushed in.

The scene was horrible. The place was drenched with German blood. In the corner of a room, a badly wounded officer was burning some papers to prevent them falling into our hands. Within seconds, the whole place burst into a raging furnace. The dead and wounded were incinerated. Neilson was scorched as he tried to rescue the papers, but it had flared so suddenly that he only just managed to get out himself. There was no hope of saving any wounded. The farm burned all day. We didn't trouble about it again.

As we were moved forward to our next position, Noel McDonald took my gun from me to give me a spell. I took his panniers of ammunition, walked around a large shell hole and turned to say something to Noel.

I was paralysed for a fraction of a second. I could not believe my eyes. My gun was sticking in the mud, muzzle first. Noel was on his back. I rushed to him, raised his head and said, 'Where, Noel, where?'

I tore open his tunic, but he just smiled faintly, pressed my hand and was gone. Cyril Palmer took his papers. I couldn't. I felt mentally dead. In a dazed way, I could see myself where Noel was. If he hadn't insisted on taking the gun from me, it would have been me there, not him. I obviously hadn't got all the snipers.

I vowed vengeance over Noel's body. But it was denied me before I could even get to my feet. One of my mates settled with the lone sniper.

We now set about digging in, two guns being sent out by each Company to cover us while we did so. Cyril and I were to cover our left wing. This required us to go about 50 yards and occupy a shell hole from which we could command a good field of fire. Our immediate front was safe from counter-attack. Two hundred yards ahead of our position, a small streamlet had become blocked at some time by shellfire. It was now a fair-sized bog that would have been impossible to walk through. We had plenty of time and Cyril and I gave our guns a hurried clean. Mine certainly needed it.

Cyril and I left our shell hole in a quick search for German rifles. We wanted to be able to do some stray sniping without wasting our own ammunition. It dawned on us to also collect ammunition from our dead mates. While we kept an eye on the front in case any Germans appeared on the hill, we had, within half an hour, each secured a German rifle and ammunition, as well as over 2500 rounds of our own. I dumped some of the rounds handy to where the boys were digging in. My final pile was very good to look at. I expected to get plenty of opportunity to direct an enfilade at Fritz before nightfall. One or two counter-attacks were sure bets.

Occasionally, Cyril had a shot at a tree just for practice with the German rifle. I teased him about his accuracy and the uselessness of a Hun gun. Suddenly a German appeared on top of the hill for a look around. Cyril grabbed the rifle, fired and dropped him. I gasped. It was a crack shot. Cyril's sights stood at 550 yards.

A few minutes later, we both got a surprise. On the lower slopes, about 500 yards away, we saw two Germans carrying a stretcher with what appeared to be a wounded man on it. We were supposed to be the lookout but we hadn't seen them until then. I watched for a few seconds and became more and more convinced that it was not a person on the stretcher. I guessed at it being a machine gun covered by a blanket. I needed to be sure.

To fire at a stretcher could be seen as firing at the Red

Cross. I asked Cyril to pull out my small field telescope from my haversack. I was still not quite certain and called over our platoon officer, Potts, to check. While he did so, I took aim. Potts hardly had time to say more than 'It's a mach . . .', when I fired. I got both men before Potts finished his sentence, '. . . let them have it.'

As the stretcher fell, a machine gun rolled off for all the world to see. I breathed a sigh of relief. My mind was easy. But behind me, the CO, Rauch, ran up yelling.

'You idiot, Sonny boy. I'll shoot you. They were stretcher-bearers with a wounded man.'

I was astonished. I whirled around and instinctively drew my revolver. Before I knew what I did, I fired two shots at him, both of which missed.

'Come on,' I yelled back. 'You dirty stinking German lover.'

But Rauch had dropped his revolver in fright. He stood there, staring at me, shaking. Potts and Cyril both grabbed me.

'Stay still, don't move,' they said.

Potts looked at Rauch. 'Get scarce.'

Rauch recovered too quickly. 'I'll get you court martialled and shot for this, Private.'

'Forget it, Rauch,' said Potts. 'Every man here saw what happened. And you know that every man here thinks like Sonny, that you're a German. If anything happens to Sonny, they'll get you. So if you want to get out of here alive, let the matter drop.'

'Come on, Rauch,' I said, 'let's both go over to the stretcher and see for ourselves. Come on.' I was mad enough to go if he would, but Rauch shook his head.

Rauch turned to go back to the trench. As he did so, we both saw two of my mates, in deadly earnest, behind the sights of their rifles pointed directly at him. He staggered at the shock of realising I was not on my own in this. Potts yelled at the men to lower their rifles. They did, very slowly, while staring at Rauch. The rest of the troops grabbed their shovels and resumed digging in.

I never heard another word spoken about the incident. Soon afterwards, Rauch left the front line. It was reported to me much later that he saw the war out at base camp at Étaples. I had known Rauch at Armentières. Even then, several of us had suspicions about where his loyalty lay. I had witnessed and heard of times when he seemed to divert our troops from action against the Germans. But if it were true, he had been too shrewd to actually betray himself. Those thoughts were instantly back in my head when I swore at him.

The trench layout was finalised and we were all called for check-in. But the ground was so muddy that the trench kept sliding in on itself. We stacked more and more bits of shattered timber against the mud until the walls finally held up enough. The timber in the bottom of the trench now kept disappearing from sight into more mud. The trench was finished sufficiently just before a German reconnoitring plane flew over, quickly followed by a few shots from their artillery. Their shells burst deep in the soft ground, only splashing a bit of mud about. Fritz gave it up without damage to any of us.

At mid afternoon, Fritz began the expected counter-attack. It fell first on 2nd Auckland and the Aussies to our right. I left our trench with the gun team to take up a position about 600 yards from the German right wing, now that we could identify where they were. I had about 3000 rounds with me. I could pick out easy targets and, firing short bursts, I began to act on the vow I had taken over Noel's body.

We had six or seven of our guns firing at Fritz and began to tear his initial attack apart. Our artillery blew gaps in their ranks along the whole of their line, but still they kept coming. Germans after Germans filled up the gaps, only for us to easily take them out.

After about 20 minutes of this, their attack crumbled and Fritz fled for the heights of the hills. I had used about 1000 rounds. I had to hold fire, watch them go and wait for their next attempt.

Meanwhile, I made arrangements to move up to the right flank of Hawke's Bay Company. With the aid of willing helpers, I secured my position against snipers. I erected a barricade of timber and sandbags taken from a dugout that was useless to us. I was sure that Fritz would post snipers on the ridge overnight to try and silence our guns in the early morning and I wanted good protection. I completed my job and took a rest while I had the chance.

Their second attack came at 4pm. But my gun was now cool. I had cleaned it and it felt in beautiful order. I wanted to get down to tin tacks straight away. If Fritz succeeded with this attempt, it would give him a whole night to consolidate his position. And we had to prevent that at all costs.

Fresh reinforcements for the Germans poured over the ridge in front of us and I decided to hold my fire. The Germans were a poor target with the sky behind them. I waited until the face of the hill gave them a background. I opened my fire, emptying one drum in a single burst. When I gave a short burst from the second drum, it jammed. It took nearly a minute to clear the expanded cartridge case, and I was at it again.

I gave Cyril the gun for a while to give me a quick rest. My shoulder was sore and I knew that he was as eager as I was to keep paying off a score. Our concentrated fire from four guns at this end played havoc with Fritz. We wiped out their right wing, their remaining men fleeing. This broke up their attack and we lengthened our range another 200 yards towards the German left wing. We could see that the Aussies were being hard pressed. The fleeing of the German line in front of us probably saved them on their end. The whole German attack now gave in very quickly.

That night, the Aussies sent us their thanks. It was as good as a VC apiece to know that they recognised and appreciated what we had done.

We had been told to expect our relief to arrive after dark, but they did not. At dawn next morning, I again took up my position in my gun possie. I settled down to wait, expecting another, even heavier counter-attack any time. It did not come straight away.

Instead, stretcher-bearers appeared and came and went at will. From the way they acted, it was very likely that dozens of German wounded had drowned in the water-logged shell holes or had been smothered by the mud. The conditions around us had been muddy enough before the attacks, but the steady rain during the night had made no man's land an impassable quagmire between us. Because of this, I hoped that Fritz had given up hope of another attack. But I didn't know his persistence. I was fired up but tired and hungry. Sleep was impossible. I was covered in mud from head to foot. If I saw a blob of mud moving near me, I knew it was one of our men. I could no longer see the colour of their uniforms or mine.

At 9am, Fritz fired a solid barrage at us. Their shells went deep into the mud before bursting and did us little harm. After 15 minutes, their infantry attacked again. I was glad of the barricade around me. Two other gun teams had built barricades during the night and the three groups of us let go at the German right flank, again cutting them to shreds.

My mates and I soon stopped and looked at each other.

It was cold-blooded murder shooting at the Germans. They couldn't get through the mud and were stuck there, like rabbits in a trap. Their attack failed before it really started. The mud was worse than our bullets. When the Germans realised we had stopped shooting at them, they collected their wounded and buried their dead as best they could. I sat and watched.

The watching turned into waiting, with what patience I could, for our relief to arrive. To give ourselves something to do, we turned our machine guns on any German observation planes that appeared. None were brought down but we forced the planes to fly high, away from us.

As night fell, our flares soared into the darkening sky. Our position was safe and our new front line was established.

An hour and a half later, we were relieved by the Duke of Wellington Regiment, 24 hours late. Fortunately, our ammunition party had topped them up. It was just as well. I only had about 200 rounds left that I could give them and go back empty.

At midnight, we reached our billets and immediately received a double issue of rum. It knocked me bandy on my empty stomach. For two days standing, I had only eaten biscuits on the line. I now ate the equivalent of two teas, two dinners and two breakfasts. I slept heavily.

Our battalion had captured 10 German machine guns and over 200 prisoners. I had no idea how many we must have killed, but I knew it was many hundreds. Our company had lost 38 men, 30 killed by snipers. We had established our objective and were within 600 yards of Abraham Heights.

As I waited in the billets, I kept in touch with what was happening on the front. Because there had been no resistance, we had wanted to carry on and secure the heights, even if it had meant advancing through the mud. Our signallers asked the artillery to extend their range to enable us to advance. Our contact plane received the same request. It soon returned from artillery headquarters and dropped a note saying that the advance was not granted — it would upset further plans.

I and others were furious when we heard this. It was a disastrous policy. It gave Fritz at least three clear days to reconsolidate a position that we had effectively wiped out. It would have been absolutely impossible for Fritz to resist if we had advanced, and a sheer waste of our men and shells if we didn't.

Because the German counter-attacks had failed, they set to work with a will to wire their front. And they made sure of it. They erected two deep sets of barbed wire, one on the lower slopes and one halfway up the hill. They then dug in on the brow of the ridge. This gave them a magnificent field of fire and an impregnable position at this time of the year. They could look straight into our front line, our supports and reserves. It was folly to move about in an upright position. It meant a bullet in the head. Fritz had some very accurate snipers.

For each of the next four days it rained without ceasing for more than two hours. We were supposed to clear the ground and build up the trenches. It was impossible. The rain and mud got into everything that a German bullet didn't. We were pulled back into supports.

On the 9th October, without the New Zealand Division, the Battle of Poelcapelle was launched from the frontage we had secured on the 4th. It was intended to push the front to the foot of Passchendaele village before a later attack was expected to take the village itself. But the artillery fire was too light and we soon heard that the troops hardly got going before being pulled back. Their losses were heavy. Some who had got close to the village had to abandon the gains.

We were now very short of artillery. The ground was so muddy it was impossible to move any heavy equipment forward. We couldn't even get the pack animals through. Some of the donkeys disappeared into the mud as if it were quicksand. No man's land was now a mass of shell holes full of water and old wire entanglements, and the bodies of our men, some possibly still alive, that we hadn't been able to collect. If we could get through that in the torrential rain without artillery cover, we had to face the thick belts of German wire, pill-boxes and machine gun posts. They could see our every move.

I thought we had missed our opportunity. It made more sense to consolidate our positions. It was not to be. We were told there would be another advance soon. I did not know when this next thrust would come off, but because Fritz had been given so much time and the conditions were so atrocious, I fervently hoped I would not be in it. And nor was I.

On the night of 11th October, the Rifle Brigade, the 'Dinks', relieved the Tommies who had relieved us. They had marched several miles through driving rain. We realised they had been given less than two days to prepare. At 5.25am next morning, the 12th, a new attack, the first Battle of Passchendaele, was launched at the Germans.

And God knows how they did it, forging through mud knee deep, but some actually reached the first line of barbed wire. Our artillery hadn't been strong enough to blast a single gap in it. The wire was in such good order that the Dinks had to cut their own path through. But that slowed them down. Many died, hanging on the barbed wire. Just as had happened to the Germans days earlier, our wounded were drowned in shell holes or smothered in the mud.

When we heard that the Dinks had reached the wire,

every mother's son of us took our hats off to them. I felt proud of them and not for nothing. It might have been a failed advance but I saw it as an honourable one, given what they were up against. It beat me how not one, but dozens of them managed to reach the wire at all.

We soon heard how disastrous the stunt had been. In just a few hours, our New Zealand Division had lost over 3000 men, with over 1000 killed. Many men disappeared under the mud. We were stunned and helpless. Our men had been consigned to a pointless sacrifice.

The Canadians in reserve took over the front line, and we moved up into reserve. Dugouts were impossible. We devised what shelter from the weather we could. We collected shattered timber and pieces of roofing iron from among a heap of bricks near us that had once been a farmhouse and outbuildings bordering the Ypres-Wieltze-Passchendaele Road to Gravenstafel.

As well as erecting shelters, we gave the stretcher-bearers a hand. It was damned hard work. The mud was so heavy, it took six of us with a stretcher a good hour to travel a mile and a half. After just two trips, I was so tired that I dropped in the bottom of the trench and slept. It became common to have to dig five or six of us out during the night when a shell blew the trench in on top of us. Not many were wounded or even hurt, thanks to the deep mud.

The Germans allowed our stretcher-bearers to take out a wounded man or return empty, but they fired on us when we attempted to go into the field with an empty stretcher. The Germans clearly aimed to wound, not to kill, unless the first warning was ignored. Once, I saw two of our men, who ignored the warning, shot at. Both were killed. It might have been a strange thought to have under the circumstances, but I felt that Fritz was justified.

For a few days, I was back in billets. The mood among us was despondent. We were exhausted. We knew we had suffered a major defeat and lost some very good men and officers. None of us had wanted to experience that. There was a morale that we started to refer to as 'before Passchendaele', and one that we referred to as 'after Passchendaele'.

Chapter 9

Ypres, 1917–1918

The whole front settled down to comparative quietness — except for the planes. Aerial battles, sometimes on a large scale, became frequent. The Germans had the upper hand in the air and they carried out daylight bombing raids over every part of the sector and into the countryside beyond. Roads, railways, ammunition and supply dumps, water tanks, rest camps and horse lines all suffered from their share of the bombs. Our battalion transport was practically wiped out in one of the raids.

Our own aircraft were very much inferior in numbers and seemed powerless to prevent the raids. For them to attack the German planes meant sure death without even a fighting chance. And as for our anti-aircraft guns, Fritz ignored them. Their general plan was simplicity itself. Half a dozen fast planes would draw the fire of our guns while some bombers would work around well out of danger and come in at our rear. Our guns would have to cease firing or be seen and get blown to pieces by the bombs. Their main bombing party would then be left clear to do their damage further afield. They would drop a huge load of bombs and nearly always survive to return home for another bout.

They carried out these tactics three or four times a day when visibility was good. Yet for all this clever work, they registered few direct hits. Fritz always seemed to be in a feverish hurry to get away. Getting rid of the bombs was probably the main idea. Just as well for us. A great deal of general damage was done but it would have been so much worse if Fritz had taken his time.

I was on salvage fatigue heading towards a large shell dump beside the Ypres and Gravenstafel Road nearly half a mile away, when it received a direct hit. I didn't wait to see the first result but dived for cover among already shattered trees. It was a steel storm. Fragments fell in all directions and a few of my mates were wounded. The explosion was so violent, that the pilot nearly lost control and looked as if he were about to crash. I dearly wanted to see him land in the centre of the dump. His plane was damaged by pieces of flying shell, but not enough for my liking and, unfortunately, he righted himself. He broke all records in heading for home.

The German scout planes sometimes came very low over our front and support lines intending to pepper us with bullets. Once, when some of us were out cable laying, I witnessed a remarkable piece of shooting, or good luck, from one of our anti-aircraft gunners about 100 yards away. Two German scouts were indulging in their pastime of peppering the line. Our gunner's first two shots blew the fuselage of the nearest plane in half. It fell like a stone between the front and support trenches, its two occupants being killed. In alarm, the second plane banked, fully exposing its body. Our gunner's third shot hit between the body and the right wing. It fell instantly into the front line, again the pilot and the observer being killed.

Everyone who had seen it gaped, incredulous. We all shouted our praise to the astonished gunner.

'I do it for a living,' he shouted back.

'Performances like that are nothing,' his lieutenant cheerfully assured us. 'He previously got five planes.'

I had my doubts, but to get two planes with three shots was something to see. But none of us had time to savour it.

The Germans suddenly turned a battery of guns on the wreckage of the planes to smash them completely. A heavier gun fired a shot at our anti-aircraft gunner. It landed short, but directly into a crowd of Ruahine Company men who had stood up to talk about the incident. That single shell killed 19 and wounded 23. It was an horrific tally that I did not hear beaten. But within seconds, a hurricane of German shells caused even more casualties. We had made a splendid target. There had been about 500 of us laying the cable and we had all reacted to our gunner's accuracy.

The ground had been covered in light snow for several days now, and the soil was frozen to a depth of about 18 inches. This hardness made the shells burst near the surface and add to the list of casualties. The Germans ceased shelling after about two minutes. It did not take us long to finish burying the cable and get out of that spot. The Germans didn't seem to care whether or not we laid cables. They must have known what we were doing. I wondered if Fritz had his eye on the cable for his own use.

This pattern of air dominance by the Germans continued for nearly two months. It only began to change when we introduced several new triplanes. We could see that Fritz was scared of them. The triplanes could climb to an angle of 45 degrees, dive nearly straight down, were fast and manoeuvrable. The numbers of German planes being brought down increased rapidly and this must have alarmed them. Our planes were now able to enter German territory with more zest.

On another day when returning from more cable laying, I paused to watch one of our 12-inch naval guns, mounted on a carriage, firing beyond the German line. An observation plane, spotting for the gun, got into the track of a shell as it was fired. The tail of the plane was ripped away by the shell. From about 1000 feet, the plane nosed straight down. The crash was terrific, the whole engine being completely buried in the mud.

A group of us dashed over, not holding out any hope for the pilot. He was just pulp. We dug him out. Although it was all over for the pilot in less than 10 seconds, I thanked my lucky stars that I didn't have far to fall.

The Hooge, Zonnebeke and Westhoek area had become familiar to me during these months as we went back and forth from the line into relief. The country further afield, near Birr Crossroads, Idiot Corner and the water tanks beside Westhoek Road, was to be avoided if possible. We never knew when shells would strike. The famous Dead Mule Gully of Ypres, a depression about 200 yards long and 30 feet high, was the entry to this area. It was aptly named. The carcasses of mules were everywhere and the smell was horrendous.

If we had to take newcomers through here, we often played a joke on them. At one time, Fritz had been in possession of this area. Two fully dressed, but very dead Germans, had been left lying on a small mound overlooking the duck walk track. Beside each corpse, a rifle had been positioned as if ready for use. At a first sighting, the impression of being in their sights was very real. We would be taking the newcomers up to the line about 2 miles further on, rifles loaded, when one of us would shout, 'Good God, it's Fritz — we're in the front line.'

The newcomers would let go a hail of bullets. And it would take a few seconds for them to get the joke. Sometimes, one or two would get annoyed at being had, but they kept the secret for later use with some fresher mug. Nearly all of us had fallen for it on our first trip past here. Each coal-scuttle helmet had dozens of bullet holes in it, and the uniforms were riddled.

Ten minutes walk from here brought us abreast of the Butte. A drearier waste was impossible to imagine. There was not a yard of solid soil anywhere. The earth had been churned up by thousands of shells. Most of the holes held frozen water. Only new holes since the last rain were dry. But the Butte was a wonderful landmark. It was perhaps 400 feet high and 200 yards long. Several of our battalion headquarters and dressing stations were located in the base of the hill and consequently, there was always someone coming or going. So Fritz shelled the vicinity three or four times an hour, turning it into a hornets' nest.

It was unpleasant and dangerous work to get a wounded man to these dressing stations, but the next nearest was at Birr Crossroads, 2½ miles further to the rear. There was no dodging it.

In front of the Butte, and stretching away to the right on a gentle slope, was Polygon Wood. With a few exceptions that had defied shells, the whole wood was just a large mass of shattered, dead trees. The effect was grim and stark. Falling away in slight dips, the wood was simply a series of small swamps. Our front line ran through these swampy patches. The slightly higher ground was held by the Germans. Directly opposite the left of the wood, were the ruins of Polygon Chateau, now a German machine-gun strongpost.

Behind, and to the left of the Butte was Crucifix Dump. It stood on what had once been a main road, cutting across country from Gravenstafel. The Crucifix was in a bad way but still standing. It was our ration dump and the furthest point to which our battalion transport could safely go — that is, after running the gauntlet over the 2½ miles of Westhoek Road which was constantly under fire. When any of us left the Crucifix with a load of rations, we would be urged on by German shells. There would be no time to stand on ceremony of any kind.

Nearly three-quarters of a mile directly in front of the Butte was J5 Central. This large concrete structure had been a German strongpost but now housed the company headquarters and cookhouse. Fritz did not waste shells on it, but once in a while fired over a shrapnel shell. Fortunately, these never caught anyone. The mud was now knee deep and it was nearly impossible to get any of the wounded along the communication trenches.

Here, the front line faced a large valley. Fritz occupied one slope and we another, leaving us generally about half a mile apart. Fritz had the advantage on us from Polygon Chateau where the valley narrowed to a neck, bringing the front lines about 100 yards apart at that point. Because we were now into winter, Fritz often left us alone. There was little to do but keep the trench in repair or mend the occasional gap blown in the wire.

Inside the German front line, perhaps a mile away, was a large village. At first, I was surprised to find that it was practically intact. When visibility improved, I could see that the village was plastered with the Red Cross on nearly every wall and roof. Yet at times, I was sure that guns fired on us variously from the edge, the centre and the rear of the village. This was confirmed when one of our planes flew over for a look and was blown to bits. Shortly after, a second plane suffered the same fate. It seemed that Fritz had no intentions of allowing a British plane anywhere near. We soon heard that two of our planes sneaked up in the early dawn and dropped hundreds of pamphlets over the village. This meant only one thing.

We set to work earthing up our dugouts to make them as secure as possible. We did not expect to see the village laid waste today because it was Sunday. But Sunday was often a moving day. In fact, recently, every Sunday was a moving day for relief of the line and other general activities. We did not want those who relieved us to say we had left the dugouts in poor condition — not that we could improve them much. And sure enough, at dusk, we were relieved and sent back to Manawatu Lines, one of our rest camps.

Two days later while on salvage fatigue around Hooge and Zillebeke, we were stopped at Birr Crossroads, the junction of Menin and Westhoek Roads. We were told that all troops and those on the front line had been ordered back. The area was crowded with heavy artillery tractors, motor trucks, horses and men. Two locomotives were waiting to haul away the 12-inch naval guns mounted on rails as soon as they had finished firing. Tractors and engineers waited to move the 15-inch howitzers. We had to wait in the open country and find what shelter we could.

The pamphlets had given the Germans 48 hours' notice to evacuate all wounded and hospitals from the village and notified them of the hour of the strafe.

Towards 11am, an awful silence settled on everyone. The anticipation was incredible. Right on the stroke of 11am, our heavy artillery unleashed its capability. The din was immediately indescribable. Shells as tall as me and weighing half a ton hurtled from the 15-inch howitzers, 1000-pound shells from the 12-inch guns, 900-pound shells from the 9.2-inch guns. The regularity of the firing was fascinating to watch. For the years I had spent here, I had not seen them in action like this. Further ahead, the 6-inch and 6.19s were firing at top speed, and beyond them the 4.5s and 18-pounders were going eyes out.

The sky was full of our planes hovering in the vicinity of the front line to drive back any German planes that might appear. Our guns had to be protected from the spying eyes of their cameras. Just off Menin Road, between Birr Cross and Hooge, a battery of six 6.19s waited in case any German observation balloons appeared. Only one did, to immediately go down in flames. I thought the 6.19, a sort of cross between a field and naval gun, was the most graceful-looking gun that ever fired a shell. It had an effective range of 32,000 yards and fired a 60-pounder. To see so many firing at once was an amazing sight.

It took Fritz 10 minutes to retaliate. He used no half measures. Menin Road began to get raked and we were moved further back. I watched Fritz getting closer and closer to one of our 12-inch naval guns. It was hauled back to a new position just as two heavy high explosives landed right where it had been. They exploded the shells left behind by our gunners.

The direct hits on Menin Road started to take a toll among the horses and men, yet few were actually killed. Even further away, Westhoek Road seemed to be in the air half the time. It was a simple target and very few shells missed.

No camera could have told in pictures what I watched. Without the terrible din, half the interest would be lost. It was a sight I could never forget. I was enthralled by its magnificence but I thanked my lucky stars that I was not in the artillery. They could not leave their guns, no matter what happened, and had to see it out as long as they were capable of standing.

At 12am, after exactly one hour, our firing ceased. Fritz kept strafing for a while, but by 12.30 there was not a gun or shell to be heard. We had to wait till 1pm before being sent out to salvage shells and equipment. In fact, we collected anything we could move. Our salvaging took us among the batteries placed between Hooge Crater and Zonnebeke. Twice during the afternoon, Fritz strafed the guns. We had to leg it for all we knew how.

I supposed that Fritz was still a bit upset at our attack.

We also encountered several of our artillerymen from the light field guns being led along the duck walk track by mates. Fritz had put down a heavy barrage of mustard gas on the field guns. Every man being led out was stone blind. There must have been 30 at least. They were fairly cheerful. Only in very serious cases does mustard gas produce permanent blindness, so they held high hopes of getting their sight back. But seeing them, even if temporarily blinded, sent a horrible chill through me.

Blindness was one of two things I hoped to be spared on the battlefield. The other was a slow, agonising death, alone.

But living under these conditions was too much occupied with fatigue tasks and too serious for me to keep these thoughts for long. Within half an hour, I had forgotten the artillerymen — for the time being. I stopped to talk to a mate, standing opposite me across a huge shell hole, perhaps 4 yards wide. Fritz was still shelling a battery a quarter of a mile away in front of us. Without any warning or sound, a shell landed between us, burying itself in the ground with a slight heave. We looked at each other in disbelief and took off as fast as we could. Both of us stumbled head first into another shell hole, full of stagnant water. The shell was a dud, but so was I. I came out stinking — and swearing and cursing at every German gunner I could name.

The following Sunday, we returned to the front,

occupying the line close to the village our gunners had shelled. Nothing stood. The whole place was flat except for countless heaps of bricks.

That trip on the front was uneventful. When relieved, we went to Belgian Camp for a rest, about 8 miles behind the line. The camp was only within range of the big guns and mainly too costly for Fritz to think of shelling us regularly. At times, though, shells did land among the artillery transports, causing considerable damage because of the size of the shell.

It was now snowing most days. I kept inside the huts and yarned with mates, played cards, hunted for body lice or scratched myself at intervals. We all had scabies. There was no water to wash with in the front line. Although there was plenty in the shell holes, it was foul or poisoned by gas. Even going to collect water in the camp required taking a bayonet. The nearby creek was frozen with a good 6 inches of ice on it.

In each hut, braziers constantly burned to heat our water for shaving. We washed with carbolic or Lifebuoy soap in an endeavour to cure or at least check the scabies.

Our yarning was not fit for any drawing room, yet anyone who became too lurid was immediately silenced. A certain poor air of decency was maintained.

On my first visit to the dental clinic in the CCS at Dickebusch, I saw something that greatly shocked and surprised me. As was usual, the railway line ran alongside the clearing station. About 80 yards to the left of the hospital stood two marquees, marked 'Isolation, keep away'. There were two large Red Crosses were on the roof of each tent. But I noticed that a small branch of the railway went into each tent, although the rail lines were camouflaged. I was nosy about the unusual nature of this. I looked inside the first tent.

I was dumbfounded. A 12-inch naval gun was mounted on a carriage with a stack of shells nearby. I looked in the other Red Cross tent. It housed a similar gun.

I had been in France over 18 months. This was the first time that I discovered that our people, too, resorted to such a low and despicable stunt. It stunned me. Hundreds of times, many of us had run the Germans down for such an act. We had just blown a village apart because of it.

When I returned to camp, I told my mates. I was called a liar without hesitation. I told them where they could see for themselves. Several made the trip on purpose the next day. They returned, their faith sadly shaken in the squareness with which we used to boast was our method of fighting. Two guns, or a hundred, hidden this way made no difference. The fact remained that we misused the Red Cross.

Sometime later, I heard that Fritz had shelled the Dickebusch CCS, blowing up one of the guns. The other had been hauled to safety. I could only guess if Fritz was after the gun or taking revenge on the hospital.

Further to the south-west of us, near Bailleul, were two compounds side by side that we sometimes visited while on rest. One of the compounds held the Chinese labour parties, and the other held German prisoners.* The prisoners were collected from the different sectors. If information could be got from them it was, or the prisoners would be passed to other compounds. While in the compound, the prisoners were under armed guards, although that often seemed unnecessary. None of them were eager to head for Germany until the war was finished. They knew they had a good thing going. They were well treated and better fed than they had been for months — and made no secret of it.

---

* Some 95,000 Chinese labourers were brought from China to work for the British Army behind the lines in the First World War. Clad in distinctive uniforms, they were known as the Chinese Labour Corps.

I often used to try and talk with the prisoners about who would win the war. Sometimes all I got was a shrug. At other times some said they would, a few said we would, but most did not seem to care. They were safe and laughed when they said so. There were some fine-built men among them, and most of our conversations were friendly. Only occasionally, was one surly or refused to talk at all.

Every so often, Fritz tried to shell Bailleul with his long-range guns. One shell fell very short of its target and blew down a part of the fence of the Chinese compound. Naturally, the Pats scattered and a few managed to get away in the dusk before the guards could stop them.* They came back when the shelling stopped but had made good use of their short liberty. They returned with some Mills bombs. Next morning, as usual, they walked around the compound before beginning duties. The German prisoners were also taking a walk at the same time. The Pats suddenly threw the Mills bombs over the fence among the prisoners. The Germans scattered like hares.

But the Pats made one fatal mistake. They clearly did not understand the bombs and failed to pull the pins before throwing them. The bombs did not explode. The Pats realised something was wrong and started to gather, curious, some leaving the shelter of their huts to take a closer look. The Germans were no mugs. They grasped the situation in a flash and darted for the bombs. It took them but a second or two to pull the pins and let fly. The result was disastrous for the Chinese. About 50 fell victims to their own plot. Most were wounded, but some did go to see Buddha to ask what that was all for.

After a few days' rest at camp, we were again detailed for

---

* Pats, as a slang reference to the Chinese, was used in New Zealand as early as November 1910. The origin is unknown.

more cable laying. By now, this was so well advanced that we frequently worked among the guns. We worked like demons to get past them, as we often came in for heavy shelling directed at the guns. One spot was absolutely loathsome. We were working between the 6.19s and the 6-inch howitzers that were only about 100 yards apart. We were cutting down the middle when we were warned that the 6-inch guns would have a short shoot. And that meant look out for reprisals. With the guns barking furiously in our ears it was impossible to dig, so we rammed fingers in our ears and sat tight. Our guns ceased after a few minutes.

And then the circus started. Reprisals were right. I think Fritz blazed back everything he had that day. It was the hottest bit of shelling I ever fell foul of. One shell in their first salvo blew up one ammunition dump, completely blew over the gun and killed all crew. The blast knocked flat any of us still standing. Some were hit by shells and falling earth. At that moment, it seemed that all of France and Belgium was in the air.

The shells now came at us like hail. We had to get out of there. Some idiots dived under sheets of roofing iron over the dugouts and no doubt felt safe from flying fragments. But absurd as it can seem, that only hoodwinked them into thinking they were safe. The rest of us rushed from shell hole to shell hole, ducking, diving and dropping flat as shells landed close. We headed for open ground as fast as we could. Some were hit by shell fragments or shrapnel as we ran. We grabbed them and carried them with us. Some were killed in that rush. We had to leave them, knowing we would return for them later.

I expected to go out at any moment. I was so close to some of the shells that I actually saw them strike. The earth seemed to fly in all directions just before the shell struck. It was if the shell still had another foot to fall. It was uncomfortable in the extreme to be that close to falling shells. But to see them seemed safe.

When Fritz stopped, it didn't take long to find out that our cable had been blown to bits. I wasn't sorry. Several of our guns were blown out and there were about 40 casualties. We attended to them, and finished the day on salvage fatigue before returning to Zillebeke.

We headed across country for Westhoek Road, listening out for the occasional shelling. We saw a dispatch rider some distance away on the road weaving among the shells falling around him. From where we were, it looked as if he was having an exciting time of it. Suddenly, his front wheel buckled under him. He shot over the handlebars like a comet and landed in the mud on the edge of the road. Before any of us could head his way, he jumped up, turned over his now useless machine, unstrapped his dispatch bag and started to leg it towards us. Almost immediately, a shell fell just behind him. He was knocked over a second time. We all chorused 'poor devil' for we did not expect to see him get up. In two seconds, he was limping across the open country to meet us. We were about 50 yards apart, when he dropped.

He had a nasty thigh wound. A big hole of missing flesh left the bone exposed. He was obviously shell-shocked and began to mutter at us. We bounced him around among us, cursed him for being a rotten coward and gave his face a couple of hefty slaps. Roughening him up had the desired effect. He calmed down but refused to let our stretcher-bearers touch him until his dispatches were on their way. One of our corporals agreed to deliver them for him.

During the next days, we were taken to fatigue duties on the light railway as far as Birr Crossroads. We caught the train there again on our return to camp. One afternoon, as we huddled up in the open truck trying to dodge the driving sleet, the train stopped for no apparent reason. We were cold and cursed the driver for mucking us around. The driver, an Aussie, got out of the engine. He walked into the dead but standing trees bordering the railway line. He took out his pocket-knife as he strode purposefully through the sleet. He stopped in front of a tree. And we saw why.

A little Tommy, almost fainted and absolutely blue with cold, was tied to the tree in such a way that he could not move. The Aussie cut him loose and held him so that he would not fall. A second lieutenant came out of the huts of the camp situated here. He saw what the Aussie was doing and shouted back into the hut. Five others and a captain rushed out demanding to know what the Aussie thought he was up to.

By this time, a group of us were out of the trucks and on the run to help the Aussie. It was clear we were all in a bad frame of mind at such a cowardly thing for anyone to have done to the Tommy. I was ready for murder and doubted it would even stop there. We all started shouting at once. We knew the Tommy was there for a punishment, but he had been freezing to his death. There was no need for this, whatever his crime had been.

One of our officers calmed us into silence. If he had called for any armed assistance from us, he would have got it. But he kept his head with us and with the British captain. He insisted that the Tommy, who was too numbed to even raise his head or his hand, be carried inside a hut.

In the mêlée, we learnt that the Tommy had struck a corporal who had been bullying him. His commanding officer had ordered two hours' field punishment, No. 1 (which meant being tied to a post with your arms bound behind your back). The Tommy had already been in the sleet for over an hour when we arrived. We gave full rein to our opinions of that commanding officer and that punishment as we boarded the train.

I had one more uneventful period on the front line before our whole division was relieved and sent for a rest back in France at Staple, between Bailleul and St Omer.

I was not in the least bit sorry. I had been six months at Ypres. It was March, 1918. It was still three months before I turned 20. And I was thoroughly tired out.

Chapter 10

Staple, 1930

The village of Staple had been just beyond the war zone. Our billets had been on a farm just outside Staple. I remember the two or three weeks here were pleasant and comfortable, with lots of water, fresh vegetables, including of course, Brussels sprouts. I thought that was appropriate, having just left Belgium. I'll wander the mile towards the farm shortly, but I first want to find a special estaminet.

Staple is easy to walk around, still clean, and no signs that it was ever ravaged by the war. It doesn't take me long to find the restaurant and bar near the centre. I stand outside, smile and listen again.

There it is — the strains of a piano and violin. They played 'Mélodie d'Amour', night after night. That music was so good to hear — a rare treat in those days. The place was always crowded with men of our battalion. Everyone so still, listening with hungry hearts, the applause deafening. Two fairy princesses were the blushing and smiling performers. They were no older than I was. None of us drank when they played. I think every man wanted the same thing. I know that all I wanted was the music and my heart missing half a dozen beats as I watched them.

Somehow, on my first night there, I managed to work my way into favour with the madame who ran the bar. I don't remember now exactly how I did. Maybe I was getting quicker and wiser at offering my services as an 'experienced' barman. Maybe I just needed to tell some tall stories. Or maybe it was because I had met up again with Lew Stemp and we got carried away with the awe of surviving. I do remember, though, that I mixed drinks that were as deadly as what we called HE, high explosives. I'd pour in a little from each bottle that happened to be handy, and plop on a crystallised cherry for effect. When there was no music, I'd get my mates drunk rather too quickly while Madame did her best to ensure they behaved themselves.

In those days it seemed I either drank a lot or not at all. Gosh, Lew and I even undid ourselves on a quart bottle or two of rum, I think it was. He and I were faced with several logs that blocked the road on our return to camp. They shouldn't have been there but they were too big to move. We smashed the bottles climbing over them.

Our company patrol picked us up and helped us back to the billets. The next morning, Lew and I were sent off parade because we still couldn't stand up, nor keep our gas masks on during the drill, nor climb the ladders without falling. We were put to bed with a lecture — and a smile from the padre for whom I had rendered a small service many months earlier. That night, I discovered the logs were nothing bigger than the twigs of a hawthorn hedge clipped by a French farmer.

But those escapades were more than balanced by the physical training and sports matches among the platoons. In one week, the change had been remarkable. I can feel it in my body now. I was no longer the weary, mud-clung man of Ypres. The difference that fresh water and dry, clean clothes could make was so delightful.

There is another reason for me to visit the farm where our billets were. For the first time, I watched snails and frogs being reared for eating. I can still picture the woman farmer in the centre of the paddock where she kept the large frog pond, feeding them meal and bread and finely chopped raw meat. She fed the snails meal, greens and milk.

The farmer laughed at us for watching but not fancying to eat such a treat. Instead, I stole her eggs at night. Some of us raided other farms nearby for carrots, parsnips, cabbages and sprouts. I hadn't seen so many fresh vegetables for such a long time. It didn't take many nights before all the farmers had watchdogs chained at their gates.

Within days at Staple, I had become as fit as a fiddle and as happy as a schoolboy in an orchard. I loved the feel of that.

But it was here, before the end of the month, and on the same night that a major fruit and vegetable raid had been planned by a group of us, that our dreams were absolutely shattered. We were told that the Germans had again broken through on the Somme. We were ordered there with all the haste that I ever saw mustered.

I can stand on the streets of Staple more than 12 years later and still feel that regret as if it were today.

Chapter 11

Back at the Somme, 1918

We were trucked the short distance from Staple to Cassel where we immediately boarded the train for Ailly-sur-Somme, just outside Amiens. The journey was cramped and took all night and into the next morning. Within minutes of leaving the train we were again on the march. It would take two to three days at an expected 15 to 20 miles a day to reach our destination.

And did I thank those few weeks at Staple. The training stuck to us. Because there was no transport, we had to carry the bombs, machine guns and ammunition. Of course those of us in the 'suicide gang', as we machine gunners were called, took it in turns with those in the 'suicide club', as the bombers were called, to give each other a spell. But it didn't make a lot of difference — each of us also carried a full pack weighing 90 pounds.

The first night, we stopped to camp in an open field. The fine weather lasted just long enough for us to get settled. As the rain started, two haystacks beside me disappeared as if by magic. My mates weren't slow. Within minutes, I too was on my groundsheet under a liberal cover of hay. It was warm and nearly as good as a roof. I slept until bugle call. The sun was rising and I smelt as fresh as the morning. The field around me looked rather like it would have at hay-making season. There were little cocks and heaps of hay in all directions with men appearing from under them.

Our smiles were interrupted by the arrival of an angry French farmer. He danced around in every direction, pointing wildly to his field. He could not speak a word of English. Suddenly, none of us could speak a word of French. After an amused standoff by us, our officer in command decided to choose diplomacy. He gave the farmer a signed order to send to headquarters for payment for his loss of haystacks.

We discovered quite quickly after the farmer had disappeared that our officer had signed the order from a mythical Australian 7th Division. We admired our CO's joke, but were disappointed that we would never get to know how the farmer fared.

The day was warm and we marched from 6am to 9pm, covering 24 miles. We were a tired lot when we stopped. But my thoughts were full of the saddening spectacle of the afternoon. We had passed hundreds of refugees, faces dead as if all hope had gone. A few tried a brave smile at us but managed only to grimace. They were either women or the young and old — too young to serve France in the war, or too old to have been considered. My heart ached at the sight of the old women especially.

The long line of refugees contained the usual vehicle piled high with household goods. Some refugees led cows and horses, others drove a few sheep. Small children, most of them crying, clung to mothers or older sisters. The old men plodded along as if impelled by sheer willpower. There was certainly no desire among any of them to have left their homes behind. I kept thinking that for the old men and women this was their time of life to rest and take comfort from the hard years of toil in their country. I was actually glad when the last of them had gone by — but the pictures stayed with me until I slept.

About midnight, we were quickly ordered out and on the road again. I was half-asleep on my legs. As dawn broke on the 26th March, we passed through and halted just outside the village of Colincamps. We were warned that Fritz was in the vicinity. Our scouts headed out to have a look. The rest of us prepared for a short stop while our officers palavered on the situation. The stop was too short. The scouts were back quickly. The Germans were marching along the road, half a mile away, towards us.

The skipper gave us orders to stand by. He then spoke those words that make any soldier face hell 10 times over and never think of saying die.

'Well, boys, it's up to us. There's no one behind us for miles — but there soon will be.'

We all knew this was bluff as other troops were days away, but the skipper continued.

'I want this crowd stopped here, right here, and knowing you, I have faith in you. Now go to it.'

No more orders were necessary. We all knew what was required. Like clockwork, we fell into extended battle order. We waited just inside the cover of the trees for that word which would take us back into action. Our platoon officer lay beside me. I knew what that meant. I could now see the Germans, less than 300 yards away. They were coming towards us in great style and pace.

The officer said in my ear, 'Sonny, you can start the ball. Fire.'

I instantly pressed my trigger and kept it pressed. Firing burst out all along our line. Germans dropped like leaves. Some initially fled in panic with us on their heels for the first few hundred yards. Fritz soon recovered and started to hold his ground. After 20 minutes, my machine-gun team was ordered back 200 yards to cover our rear in case of a gap through casualties in any part of our line. That was the worst part, as I now had to sit back and watch my mates working on Fritz. And this they did thoroughly. There were no gaps. Our boys held and gained ground slowly but surely, capturing machine gun after machine gun. There were no shells. It was infantry against infantry, and basically every man for himself.

Our objective was some old trenches, three-quarters of a mile from Colincamps. We had covered half that distance before Fritz rallied. It took another three hours to gain the rest of that objective. Our team was able to get back into the fighting, even though we had to cover our rear. It became a game of hide and seek, shoot and bolt from one bit of cover to another. We would pause in a piece of cover, fancy we were okay, then find ourselves surrounded and have to fight our way out. It would start all over again.

We soon discovered why those Germans fought as they did. It was no wonder we had our work cut out when they rallied. They were members of the Prussian Guard, Germany's crack regiment.

We took several prisoners and this became a serious handicap to our strength. Sergeant Ford took 14 single-handed and passed them down the line. Unfortunately, I saw one of our greatest Maori warriors, Dick Savage — not to be confused with Dick Travis, who was known as Savage, of the 2nd Otago — killed just before Fritz finally gave in and bolted. Dick had fought as if facing seven devils, and on his own took a huge toll of Germans. Given the open nature of the scrapping, it was surprising that we didn't suffer greater casualties. We did not even have the protection of clover for we had to keep pretty low. But we had the drop on Fritz who had to fire through his men as they gave ground. This forced their machine gunners to move frequently on to slightly higher ground. This gave us a chance to clean up party after party as they tried to save their guns when they fell back.

The German plan of massed formation didn't help them. They instinctively bunched together. Our men were from 5 to 7 yards apart. This gave my team the odd chance of shooting between our own men. It was risky, but to help them we had to take it, placed as we were behind them. It worked well. I was able to silence nine machine guns this way from our rear. I had also used up most of my ammunition for my .45 revolver.

Together, we captured 108 machine guns that day, not to mention trench mortars and several prisoners. The tally seemed incredible.

When we reached the slight rise of La Signy Farm, we halted in case of a counter-attack. We were tired, but so were the Germans. They had covered a lot of ground going backwards since the initial attack. They had lost the day, but they had fought every bit as hard as we had.

We now set about making our gain secure and preparing the sound machine guns we had captured. We collected all the ammunition possible for them. They were better than our Lewis guns, being supplied with belts that held 250 rounds. The drums of our Lewis guns held only 48. Not until both sets of guns were ready for action did we dare take a rest.

Because we had been trained to use the German guns, we were now able to split our teams in two. Instead of four guns per company, we now had eight. Other German guns were also set ready for firing by men chosen for the job. They simply had to press the trigger and keep firing.

When Fritz counter-attacked early in the afternoon,

West Coast Company was able to bring 14 guns into action immediately. The nearest any German got to our trench was a chain and a half. As expected though, six of the 14 guns went out of action as soon as one belt was fired. The men handling them were not able to reload and carry on. But the first vital shock of the attack was broken and the remaining guns were more than sufficient to cope.

Soon after this failure by Fritz, a battery of German field artillery started to shell Colincamps. One of the first shells to strike the village unfortunately killed Brigadier General Fulton and some of his staff.* He was a highly respected commander and a huge loss to the Rifle Brigade. It was one of those random events in war. The Germans were clearly just range finding. Very little other shelling was done. It seemed that the German infantry had practically run away from their artillery.

During the day, a German cyclist rode straight into our arms before he realised where he was. He was prevented from escaping with a bullet to his shoulder, splintering the bone. He carried several papers and orders but they were of no practical value. We already knew as much as the information told us. The papers also included some minor details about our reinforcements and that we had no artillery.

Shortly afterwards, a German transport wagon came down the same road towards us. We held fire. It was evident that the driver was not sure where he would meet the troops he was looking for. For some reason we could never understand, the German infantry had allowed him to drive right into our lines. The horses were brought down with a quick burst of fire. The driver was so frightened that he sat down on the road yelling, 'Kamerad, Kamerad!'

---

* Brigadier General Harry Townsend Fulton, CMG, DSO, Croix de Guerre, was 49 at the time of his death. He actually died of concussion the following day while being taken to the CCS at Doullens.

He was captured but we had to wait until dark to go near the wagon. It hadn't been a trap. The wagon gave up two machine guns, five boxes of ammunition and lots of rations.

The delay in any further counter attack gave our artillery a chance to appear by the next day. But it did not — and nor did it the next day. We began to think they must have got lost or got cold feet. In fact it took until the 2nd April for them to arrive and fire a shot.

In the meantime the inevitable rain started in earnest. It did not take long and the trenches were knee-deep with mud. After two days of getting wetter and wetter, we were relieved at dark on the 29th March by the Rifle Brigade. We were sent back to billets a mile from this line. The scarcity of artillery made that possible.

Our billets were in the outbuildings of a farm that until then had not been hit by a shell. We were surprised that it was still occupied by the farming couple. That situation lasted until morning. We all left the farm in a hurry when a shell fell just short. Inside an hour, the farm was a smouldering heap of bricks. It now looked more 'genuine'. The farmers hitched a couple of horses to their wagon that was already loaded in case, and beat a hasty retreat from the area. So much for our arrival on their farm.

We spent the day digging the 'Purple Line' which was supposed to serve as a reserve trench. We occupied it at night and continued to dig for the next three or four days. We went to Sailly-au-Bois, just north of Colincamps, in search of iron, wood and hay to make time more comfortable in the shallow dugouts. The village had been partly shelled previously. As a few of the men lifted a pile of hay from a loft, there was a sudden release of gas from within the hay. That stopped that plan. Obviously, Fritz had used gas shells on the village.

Because it was now deserted, we searched the remaining houses for old mattresses and other luxuries.

On 1st April, Fritz started to merry things up and we began to expect an attack. As the day wore on, we became more certain that they would make another bid for Paris. I could not make out why they had not already tried. They knew we had no artillery. Yet they kept up a heavy bombardment from 8am until 4pm before they turned it in. Their infantry never attempted to leave their trenches. With such an intense bombardment, the only reason could be to try and break the nerves of our troops in preparation for a big push forward. We waited.

On the next day, we again took over the front line, relieving the Dinks at dusk. The trenches were now an awful mess. No one seemed to have bothered. We had no materials to work with and could do nothing to better them.

During the afternoon, our field artillery eventually arrived. They immediately let Fritz know. But because the Germans had not had time to work out our artillery's exact location, they tried to take it out on us in the trenches. Their shooting was bad and had little effect. My team was moved to aeroplane guard.

About 300 yards behind our line and directly opposite La Signy Farm was a mixed ammunition dump. It contained .303 ammunition, 18-pounders and 4.5 shells, Stokes mortar shells, plum duffs and Mills bombs. Our aeroplane guard positioned us in a dip beside the road, about 100 yards from the dump. A German reconnoitring plane came over our lines but initially out of range. It turned heading for home and passed directly overhead, about 150 feet up. We pumped four drums of bullets into it as hard and as fast as we could. Every tracer showed that the firing was accurate, yet the pilot and observer ambled on at about 80 miles an hour as if taking no notice.

We were suddenly knocked flat from the concussion of a terrific roar, canting the post on which the Lewis gun was mounted. For a second or two, I thought the plane had dropped a bomb at us. As we got to our feet, I realised it had been the other way around. The plane had gone straight into the dump. The air was filled with everything we could imagine from earth and shells and plum duffs flying skyward in all directions. One look was enough. We dived for shelter. For a moment, nothing fell. Then it came in shower after shower of metal. I wished we had piled tons more mud on top of the dugouts.

When I ventured out, the ground resembled a shingle bed. But instead of stones, they were lumps of steel. There must have been a hundred tons of explosive matter in the dump. The hole was big enough to bury two large houses and then some.

In the middle of the metal rain, I had seen a man falling to earth. It seemed that he had been closest to the dump when the plane hit, on top of an old shed pulling iron from the roof for his dugout. He was wounded in about 40 places, all small, but his back looked like a sieve. Later, several men in the front line said that shells fell a mile away, some having gone to terrific heights. None of us was killed, but about 43 were wounded.

Fritz thought that moment ripe for a hurried raid on our front line. Fifteen Germans headed into no man's land. Fortunately, our men stayed alert. None of the Germans survived such a rash act, not even getting halfway. They didn't try again.

For the next couple of days, trench life was quiet and occupied with repairs. We were relieved by 2nd Otago and went into reserve at Sailly-au-Bois. Although a fair-sized village, it was very much damaged and totally deserted. The

Germans continued to shell it repeatedly, hoping to catch our transports that had to pass through the village to serve this part of the sector.

Our division occupied territory from Hébuterne to Mailly-Maillet, a distance of 2½ miles. The line was thinly held. In fact, our defences consisted of the front and support lines, with a couple of battalions in reserve to a division. It was not enough.

We made camp at Sailly-au-Bois among some very old artillery dugouts that had probably existed from early in the war. They had hardly been used since. Our CO arrived at our camp with a pleasant surprise for us, leading a cow in full milk through the desolation of the village.

The following morning, we marched about 2 miles to Bus-les-Artois for a bath. During the trip, several of us acquired some fowls we found wandering in an open paddock. On our return to Sailly-au-Bois, we rummaged among the remains of some homes looking for cellars. Wine proved to be plentiful. And so were sore heads next morning. But we had fed and drunk well.

Now that we had a cow, we had to feed her — and guard her. Others of our troops wanted a share of Duchess, for so we named her. A few of us raided the nearby horse lines and fodder dump. Each of us brought back a bale of good clover hay. We extended our gathering practices. Several of the shelled homes had substantial gardens. After we had collected what vegetables we wanted, Duchess got the remains of the cabbages, carrots and parsnips. And what grass we could pull was given to her. I had never seen a cow eat so much rubbish. I felt sure that she could well eat one of us, boots, uniform and all, before going hungry.

But after three days, Duchess started to become a problem. We were continually on the hop to keep her fed. She cleaned out our stock of vegetables overnight when her bodyguard went to sleep on the job. Before going back into the line, we milked Duchess dry, bade her farewell and handed her over to some of the artillery. Unfortunately, she was hit by a shell soon afterwards. The battery was furnished with fresh beef for a couple of days from what was left.

I had begun smoking and had collected a good stock of cigarettes before leaving Staple. Yet by the end of a week here, not one of us in the battalion had a packet of cigarettes left. It fell to the padre to hunt up smokes for the men. He set out on his quest but did not return until next morning. After a 20-kilometre journey, he had enough for two cigarettes each and one match.

Some of the men were so desperate that they pierced the butt of each cigarette with a pin so that they could get one or two more draws without burning their fingers. When the butt fell from the pin, it was put out and saved. A collection of these shreds provided just enough tobacco to make another small butt and give a few more draws.

The next day, the padre was off again. He had to travel 30 kilometres to the outskirts of Amiens before he had luck. He returned with enough smokes for two packets each and one box of matches between two. We were very glad to see him but offers of payment offended the padre. He insisted that payment was on the Salvation Army because cigarettes were now so hard to procure.

It had been many months since any fighting in this area. All the canteens that did exist were now in the hands of the Germans and about 5 miles behind their front line. When the Germans had broken through, the Tommies had left everything and taken off for home or Paris as fast as they could. One German officer who we had captured compared the Tommies' flight with the speed of hares. That description became a stock joke on the Tommy for a while. I enjoyed hearing the joke repeated. During their retreat, a Tommy comes across a hare also heading for safety. The hare keeps getting in the way. The Tommy gets annoyed and shouts at the hare, 'Get out of the way and let a man past that can run.'

The Germans had advanced nearly 20 miles, retaking Bapaume without much trouble. Then the British stampede began. Wherever the Tommies got to on their retreat was a mystery. They left a gap over 5 miles wide. Several of their field guns were captured. The Tommies, or 'Hares' as we now dubbed them, did not take time to bring up their horses to haul the guns away. Hundreds of tons of material, thousands of shells and nearly all their machine guns were captured by the Germans.

I often heard the claim that the British Army does not retreat — it retires. It was only a nicer word. Thank God we had the navy to fall back on. Yes, I knew that the whole British Army was thoroughly war-torn. Every man was tired mentally and physically. After four years, there was no more prospect of victory than there was in August 1914. And it seemed there would be no prospect for years to come. The force of arms, that 'might is right', was not looming on any horizon. I was seeing the war now as a question of morale, of who could stand the strain the longest. And the times I knew how close I was to cracking seemed to be increasing. I hung onto the discipline that I knew my mates and I had for ourselves.

It was probably not surprising that the army had started to flood us with stories of cruelty and persecution by the Germans against our prisoners. We were told of victories in battles that had not taken place, of trials of German war leaders and of the Kaiser. We were told of the German boiling-down factories where they took our dead to extract fat from the bodies for war purposes. The stories were supposed to keep us going, but I recognised them as unforgivable lies and sheer nonsense.

I had my own stories, though, about those French and Belgians who showed little gratefulness for our presence when we were on the march, desperate for water or rest. I sometimes wondered if it was worth going 5 yards out of our country to fight for them, let alone 12,000 miles. I had begun to think that we were all here under a falsehood, and a rather gigantic one at that. Britain had looked for an excuse to enter the war and had found it in the German breaking of Belgian neutrality. But France would have broken that neutrality, and intended to do so, so we learned while fighting here, and England was a part of French plans.

I couldn't do much with my thoughts. I could only get on with the job we were given.

My machine-gun team had to cover several different positions along the front line. The end towards Hébuterne proved an unhealthy spot. Every 10 minutes, German guns shelled the village itself and raked the surrounding territory at night with machine guns. Our artillery was now at full strength, and every half an hour we returned the shelling for 10 minutes right back to their heavy guns. The thickness of the orange flashes made it a fine sight to watch.

Our team spent a lot of time locating German machine guns and then leaving it to our trench mortars to blow them out. I could look straight up the main street of Hébuterne towards Bapaume, about 12 kilometres away. Because the Germans had now occupied Bapaume, I could watch our heavy shelling of the town. To the left of Hébuterne was the fringe of some woods. Our left flank joined up here with the right flank of the Aussies.

One of our derelict tanks still stood in front of the woods a little distance from their trench. The Germans obviously thought it unusable. But the port tank gun faced the Germans and was found to be in working order by two of the Aussies. A few shells had been left beside the gun. The Aussies discovered two German machine-gun posts that they could bring the tank's gun to bear on. They waited until the next morning broke fine. It took less than a minute to blow out both German guns. The two Aussies were back in the trench before the Germans recovered from the unexpected shock. Fritz called on his artillery to finish the tank. For 10 minutes, it simply rained shells until the tank was scattered everywhere.

Because German shells fell regularly during the night, it was impossible to do any wiring. Yet we had to patrol no man's land in spite of the bullets. That meant that when we left the trench, we had to crawl, snaking from point to point, making full use of shell holes. Our position was on the edge of a slight dip, with the Germans at the foot of the opposite slope. It was possible for us to look into a sizeable portion of their communication trenches during the day. Although their supports occupied the brow of the hill, it was only after dark that they could move to or from their front line.

After one of our brainwaves, we arranged for a battery of 18-pounders to move to within 500 yards of the German front line under cover of darkness. Just as day was breaking and their working parties were making their way to the rear, our gunners fired a few shells straight into the German communication trenches. The suddenness of it knocked Fritz. By the time they came from cover, our guns had been hitched to the waiting horse teams, and pulled through the protection of the village buildings into the dip of a shallow valley behind Hébuterne, and to our rear and safety. Our

Vickers machine gunners covered the speedy retreat of our horse teams.

We repeated this stunt over several mornings using different positions each time. We could see and hear the Germans getting very mad with us because they had no chance to fire on the battery. Although it was we in the line who caught the bulk of the shells that the Germans heaved back, we enjoyed it as if it were a joke we could play on them.

It would have been possible in this part of the French countryside to bring dozens of guns into action at the gallop, had it been necessary. Most of the countryside was entirely free of shell holes. At every 100 yards in the newly dug rear trenches, there was a solid driveway, 20 feet wide, for tanks and artillery to pass through.

Those of us on the front line used to call our artillery the 'Pretty Boys' because of their smart appearance. Few of them ever looked as filthy and muddy as we had been. But I was proud of them. I always liked to have them behind me. In the whole of the British Army, including us New Zealanders, it was our artillery boys that held the record for the fastest piece of shooting. They had been able to put through 35 shells in one minute. It was not a speed that could be kept up for long, but they had done it.

During these days, two of my team and I were given one of the worst jobs possible. We were sent out to La Signy Farm, about three-quarters of a mile to the right of Hébuterne. We had to occupy a position in no man's land, a chain beyond our wire. The three of us had to stay here through the day and night in what was known as a sleeping possie. No matter what was going on, the only conditions under which we could open fire was in the event of a raid or all-out attack. If a German patrol came into sight, we had to avoid it, crawl into other shell holes, or make it back to the line taking our gun and possessions so that the Germans would not know the position had been occupied.

This job was no joke. We had even been forbidden to fire if fired on when leaving the possie. The three of us, however, had agreed to shoot first if necessary and damn the consequences.

We were able to move to and from our possie into our own bit of trench behind us during the day if we had to. But at night, this route was blocked by rolls of barbed wire in case anyone got in behind us without our seeing them. The moon was very thin and the nights were dark. For hours on end, we could hear German wirers at work only 50 yards away. The muffled tap, tap, tap of mallets and the scrape, scrape, scrape of wire nearly drove me mad. It was as much as I could do to hold myself back. I desperately wanted to crawl from shell hole to shell hole, get to them, and open fire.

Several times, when sneaking away from their patrols at night, we were challenged. Each time we waited, yards away, not daring to move, revolvers ready. Each time, their patrols passed on. Yes, it was some sweet job out there in no man's land. We had four days and nights of that on end before being relieved for the same period. We repeated this stint three times.

Several of my mates swore that I had a charmed life in the field. They said they'd go anywhere with me in preference to the NCOs. Except once, when I was a temporary corporal for only two days, I had refused stripes because of my age and because I would have been at the beck and call of others. I would have hated that. That occasion of two days was two too long.

There were many times when I felt safe and easy in my mind that I would not be killed or wounded.

But the strain got to me badly during that third stint in no man's land. I really struggled. I was running out of willpower and I wondered if I was running out of time. Much more, and I felt I would turn tail and run. And probably, I would have been court-martialled for cowardice and lined up against a wall. I wouldn't have been the first.

I think I was saved from a breakdown by an offer of leave. I was given a choice of four days in Paris or 14 in England. The choice was easy. I took the 14 days.

Chapter 12

On Leave from the Somme, April 1918

Transport from Hébuterne to Amiens was plentiful, but I had to bribe my way and change local buses several times over the 30 kilometres. I arrived at the railway station late at night. The train took me to the French coast and north to Boulogne. I headed for One Blanket Hill on the outskirts where all troops going on leave were quartered. I was issued with my one blanket. No matter the weather or the time of year, that was the issue. I never heard of any man getting a second, not even through bribery. It was usual for two or three men to join forces with their blankets to get sleep, or shiver the night out.

Towards midnight, I was awakened by bugle calls. I quickly dressed and headed for the boat to take us to Dover. We did not meet any subs and arrived just after dawn. I had to scramble for seats on the train that would take me to London. I hardly had time to settle before being accosted by small boys, some of them dressed in postal uniform, but all carrying a telegram bag and a large sheaf of telegraph forms, enquiring if I wanted to send a telegram. I didn't know a soul in England and had no use for the boys even if I had wanted to. I had heard, though, that these boys charged well for themselves at a shilling or two, and never dreamed of sending a message to anyone. There were no flies on these boys. I nevertheless watched dozens of the men using the offers.

The train arrived at Victoria Station at 10.30am. It was crowded, mainly with young women.

I couldn't believe the brazenness of a good-looking young woman who rushed up to me, threw her arms around my neck and said, 'Oh Bob, I never expected to see you again so soon.'

I was furious and none too gentle. I tore her arms away and said, 'Get the hell out of my way. I'm not Bob and I've never seen you before in my life.'

'Oh,' she said. 'I've made a mistake.'

'You bet you have and now leave me alone.'

Instead of leaving things at that, she started to abuse me for all she knew. I couldn't believe her language. I grabbed my gear and made for a taxi. The young woman turned her attention to another soldier, much to my relief.

I caught a taxi with Ernie Barron, whom I had travelled with from France. We headed for the Soldiers' Club in Russell Square. First up was a hot bath, full and with plenty of disinfectant. I took my time soaking.

I returned downstairs to the office of the club to leave the bulk of my money in safety. They ran a letter of credit system for our benefit. If I were to get robbed, I would not lose much and still have enough to fall back on. As long as I had my pass and pay book, I could draw on my deposit daily or as I chose, each amount being deducted from my total. They seemed to keep a very quick and accurate system of transactions.

Ernie and I headed for the dining room. What a treat. We sat down at a clean table, with cutlery, with a decent meal. The lady helpers were splendid. They worked hard for our benefit, referring to us all as 'the boys'.

During the afternoon, Ernie and I took a conducted tour of part of the city. It was too hurried. I felt as if we were being led around like a flock of French sheep, seeing things only from a distance and not hearing a word of what the guide said to us. It wasn't what either of us wanted and we decided to do our own tour the next day.

We spent the early part of our first night in the Alhambra Theatre, before strolling along Southampton Row towards Russell Square, enjoying the night air. We were close to Holborn Tube Station when an air-raid warning started. Everyone around us made for shelter and told us to do the same. We must have looked too casual. I was initially astonished that so few showed any panic. Their only excitement was caused by the hurried search for shelter if they found the first place full and had to find room elsewhere. Ernie and I found shelter in a basement across the road.

We hadn't been there long, when I noticed a woman, probably about 70, huddled into a corner by herself. She was dressed in her nightgown with her bathrobe tied tightly around her. Her teeth chattered and she did not look well in her eyes. She scuffed her slippers on the concrete floor and, with each foot movement, gave a little sob. It was pitiful to see. I looked around me. Others weren't at their best either, but everyone ignored her. No one tried to comfort the old woman.

Ernie had seen her. 'Hell,' he said, 'I can't leave her like that and stand here like a stone.'

He sat with her. I hadn't credited Ernie with what I saw. He put an arm around her shoulder as in a protective caress. He spoke to her with such gentle, soothing and reassuring words that I gaped. Slowly, a ghost of a smile crept into the corners of her eyes. She relaxed and began to look calm as if there were no such thing as danger in this world. She turned towards Ernie and, like a fond mother, placed a hand on each shoulder and drew him to her.

She kissed him ever so lightly on his cheek and said, 'Thank you, my son.'

They were four such simple words. The pathos of it brought hot tears into my eyes. I couldn't fight them back.

I heard Ernie say, 'Thank you, lady.'

He turned away and made for the door, even though the all clear hadn't sounded. I followed and saw that he, too, had tears running down his cheeks.

As soon as we reached the street, I reached for Ernie's hand, and shook it. 'I didn't know you had that in you,' I said to him.

'My God,' he said quietly, 'I had to get out. I couldn't have handled another minute there, even if I'd been paid for it. I haven't spoken feelings like that for ages.'

I knew he meant it and I knew he was embarrassed. We walked slowly in the darkness as Ernie told me about his wife and two kiddies in New Zealand. He clearly thought the world of them. Perhaps that explained some of what I had seen. It only explained some of what I had felt.

We were within 100 yards of the Soldiers' Club when the all clear sounded. Crowds poured from the basements. I was surprised at how many had been below ground. We stood on the steps of the club, enjoyed a cigarette and watched the mix of people hurrying home or lingering and yarning. Even young boys continued trying to sell papers. Several girls, looking younger than me, passed us and called out, 'Goodnight, digger', or, 'Coming home with me, digger?' We ignored them.

Next morning, Ernie and I spent a good hour planning a sightseeing tour of our own. We decided to start handy to the club and gradually extend our ground so that we did not have to ask for directions. The plan worked well at first. But because we were on our own, the continual 'Hello digger' from girls began to annoy me. I suggested that we might have to put up with a girl each or we would get no peace. We might find they were good guides and worth the money we might have to spend on them. Ernie agreed, but with reservations. He didn't want it to be interpreted by the girls as anything other than guiding.

While we were discussing this on the edge of the footpath, two girls sidled up almost unnoticed by us. I explained our position to them very frankly. They grinned, giggled and agreed that of course we would not want their company for longer than that afternoon.

I always tried to treat everybody as straight and honest in such circumstances. But I was too inexperienced in the ways of these women. I did not realise for one minute that my frankness would cost me. I thought their giggles meant they were tickled by my proposition.

When we reached the crypt of St Paul's, the girls managed to have Ernie and me lose each other in the crowds. I was led to some tearooms where my girl ate well. I kept looking for Ernie but was persuaded to take my girl sightseeing alone. We went to a play, to supper, to a bar and I saw her home to her place. When she invited me in, I refused, saying I would head back to the club. Again, she persuaded me that we were now miles from the club and too far to return at this hour. I had a cup of cocoa and slept on her floor.

Next morning I wanted to find Ernie and I needed more money. My girl had encouraged me to spend well. Less than a two-minute walk from the girl's place brought me into Russell Square. I had to laugh at being had.

The girl followed me, wanting to stay with me for the day, but because she was not allowed in the club, I said I would wait for Ernie in the reading room. Every so often, I peeped out the window to see the girl still there. She stuck it out for an hour before disappearing. I waited another hour. It was the last I saw of her.

I again booked my bed at the club and walked around the streets. I ran into Ernie later in the day and discovered his experience had been similar. I was pleased to see him as I had got to like him. He seemed a steady man.

Over the next few days, Ernie and I travelled to Brighton and to Blackpool. The girls were as bad everywhere. As soon as they saw khaki, they wanted to sidle up to the wearer and make his acquaintance.

Suddenly, we had only six days left. We returned to London. And funnily that night, Ernie and I started talking with two girls whose conversation we immediately enjoyed. They both had jobs near the club and invited us next day to their workplace and to lunch. We met up again at night and found we all got on very well.

When Jenny told me her birth date, I couldn't believe it. It was the same as mine. We were twins. And so Ernie and Lily dubbed us that. Quite quickly, a strong friendship sprang up between Jenny and me. She put us wise to an astonishing number of things around London and saved us a good deal of money.

For our last weekend in England, the four of us decided we wanted some quiet time together. We travelled to Epsom where we rented rooms from a Mrs Jeffries in Hook Road. Jenny and Lily took the upstairs room and Ernie and I shared the double room downstairs. Mrs Jeffries was a lovely soul and treated us as if she were our mother. We discovered that her husband was a prisoner of war in Germany and was being used as a horse trainer for the Kaiser. She kept asking when the war would end. Her four sons had been killed in France and she lived only for her husband's return. Throughout the weekend, Mrs Jeffries, Ernie and Lily kept remarking how good Jenny and I looked together.

The day Ernie and I had to catch the train to Dover, Jenny clung to me in a way I could never forget. She asked me to break my leave and stay in London where she would hide me. I had to say no. I said I had to be honest with myself. I had three years' service and would lay myself open to being shot as a deserter. I couldn't disgrace my folks at home by doing that. I asked her if she preferred to care about a deserter or a man who took his chances honourably.

When she saw that I would not betray myself or my family or my mates in France, she gave in as long as I promised to write. I promised.

I suddenly realised I was having one of the hardest battles I had fought. I had feelings of love for Jenny, even after knowing her just one week. I kept my strength and said my farewells. But until it was time to catch the train, I walked the streets on my own, knowing I was torn between desire and duty.

The run to Dover was a nightmare. I did not feel safe from jumping the train and deserting until the boat pulled out from the wharf.

As I headed for Boulogne, surrounded by our escort of destroyers, I gave no thought to submarines.

Chapter 13

More of the Somme, May 1918

When I returned from leave, the brigade was out for a short rest at Authie Wood, west of Hébuterne. I was thankful. I felt better from having had leave but torn about Jenny. I also knew that I was far from well physically and mentally. My nerves were all over the place. I jumped every time a shell struck, even when it was a mile away.

I had never questioned my ability to hold on as much as I did now. And it was not helped by what we heard during the last days of April. The Germans had recaptured Messines Ridge. They had heavily attacked Armentières with gas, causing all Allied forces to evacuate. They had reoccupied Passchendaele and had also bombarded Ypres with gas.

Authie Wood was 5 miles behind the front. Thousands sheltered under canvas. The tent floors were sunk 2 feet below the ground surface in an attempt to avoid shells and aerial bombs. We were close to a small aerodrome that was well camouflaged in the trees. The Germans knew it existed. Most nights, a couple of Gothas would have a go at it but they never managed a direct hit. Our cadets, the 'Archies', would blaze away at them and give them little opportunity to get too close. As a result, though, the night air was full of falling shrapnel. All I could do was put my pack over my head and practise grinning. I hated the aerial bombs now, more than ever I had. They were 10 times worse on my nerves than the biggest shells.

The days were quiet and taken up with a few hours of drill and practising for attack. With nowhere to go afterwards, my option was to get merry and even drunk once or twice. Some of us had found a source of liquor and, under its influence, I tried to forget where I was for a few hours at least.

After only a few days, we left Authie Wood to return to the front line at Hébuterne. This time, my luck was in. My team was detailed for an SOS possie. This was a good job and I was back with Lew and Chloride. We simply had to eat and sleep and only fire on anyone or anything when attacked. The dugout was solid. We filled in our time building two firing bays, reading, writing, yarning and making wire obstacles that could be rolled over the front of the trench to block any gaps blown in our wire. We were 100 yards from the front and left our post only to take these obstacles up to the actual line.

I tried to write to Jenny. I couldn't write about what my team was doing, or my nerves. I wrote about my time in London. I wrote to Ina in Wellington and to Mum. I didn't tell either of them about Jenny.

My team was attached to battalion headquarters while at this dugout. We took no orders from the company. Our original CO, Major McKinnon, was in hospital with bullet wounds. Mellies, a townie of mine, became the acting CO. I did not like him and the dislike must have been mutual.

One evening, Mellies ordered two of my team to go on fatigue duty. I refused to let them go. Mellies and I had a hell of a row. But I continued to refuse in spite of what he said about me. He got annoyed because my team had nothing to do but stick to our post. But I knew what to expect if I disobeyed our colonel's orders.

I left Lew in charge and headed for HQ with Mellies following. I ran into the colonel just outside the company headquarters. He jumped at me straight away, wanting to know what I was doing out of my post. I explained, with Mellies beside me. I was quietly ordered to return to my gun post. The colonel took Mellies inside. I could not resist hanging around the corner. I don't think I ever enjoyed listening to anyone being told off as much as Mellies was that night. I expected that Mellies would look for a chance to get back at me and, the very next morning, he did not hesitate to let me know that he would fix me at a later date. But later did not come for him.

My team was moved back to La Signy Farm on aeroplane guard. This part of the line was generally quiet, except when Baron von Richthofen and his 'red circus' peppered us from their planes with machine guns. They had nerve and they were magnificent pilots. Germany had reason to be proud of the Red Knight and his famous flying circus. We called them the Red Devils. They would fly at no more than 100 feet on occasions. We would blaze away with machine guns and 18-pounders. The pilots took as much notice of us as if we had sat down and watched them.

It was sad the way the baron met his death. It seemed too simple. For a short while it was thought my team might have contributed. On the 21st April, Lew, Chloride and I were on aeroplane guard while in reserve between Sailly-au-Bois and Bus-les-Artois. The day quickly deteriorated into thick fog and we decided to call off our duty.

We took the gun down and began the return to our bivvy. We had gone 10 yards when we instantly stopped together. There was no mistaking the hum of a Mercedes motor flying very low towards us. We hurriedly mounted the gun. One of the 'red circus' planes showed partly through a break in the rolling fog. I fired the contents of one drum. The tracers showed that I just missed his tail. The pilot was clearly lost for I could see him looking down over his left side, trying to pick up his bearings. But before I could remedy my accuracy, he was gone into the swirling fog.

We soon heard that a plane had crashed into some trees not far from us straight after we had fired and were told that it was Baron von Richthofen himself. But I had not seen his private insignia on the fuselage of the plane we had fired on, although that could have escaped my notice. Later that day, we were told that a Canadian, then that an Australian in a unit nearby, had shot down the baron. We also heard that a captain of the Royal Air Force claimed that his men in their Sopwith Camels had brought him down in combat. Any of these could have been the correct story. Whatever the truth, the baron was not shot to pieces. His recovered body had been hit by only one bullet.

It could seem strange to describe the Red Devils as fearless and magnificent and an honour to any country. But I was proud of our own pilots, too. I groaned every time I saw one hurtling to the ground and I would yell with joy whenever a German plane was downed.

I heard comments that claimed our aeroplanes were of little use in the war and of negligible use to us in the infantry. But anyone who thought that must have had their experiences turn their brain. The flying corps was responsible for reproducing in detail the maps of the ground over which we had to go. The corps took photos of German guns for our guns to knock out, lessening the artillery fire through which we had to go. The corps located strongposts and other obstacles for us, kept in contact with us on our stunts, bombed and machine gunned Fritz when we were held up by defences not smashed by our artillery, and did the same with German reinforcements that might check our progress. They enabled many of our efforts to be successes and far less costly than they might have been.

I was noticing that I was not the only one feeling the strain. It seemed to be telling on all ranks. I didn't hear anywhere any man who wasn't now fed up with the war. Some were so fed up that they began willingly exposing themselves to machine-gun bullets to get injured. They of course did not expose the whole of their bodies, but just their arms or legs. I even saw one man stand on his hands in the trench with both legs pushed over the top. No matter how hard some tried, very few were injured in this way. A few men even injured each other deliberately. German rifles and ammunition were plentiful for this task.

I got caught up in one incident of deliberate wounding for a bet. One of the men in the platoon took me aside. He bet me 20 francs that I was not game to shoot him in the thigh. A bet was enough for me to call any bluff, if that was intended. I reached for a rifle and checked with him that he wanted me to do this. He said I wouldn't be game, even for the bet. I asked him again. He said I wasn't game for an answer. Before he could back out, I shot him in the thigh. He paid up like an honest soldier and was soon on his way to hospital, a happy man. I could only have injured him because there were only the two of us. I didn't repeat it for anyone else, but I did see it done to another.

The story of the German boiling-down factories was another strange form of desperation. It became a regular topic. I did not believe it, but some did. We made a jest of it at those going out on patrol.

'Be careful, you might finish up in a pot.'

'Watch out, you could come back as a shell.'

'Hey, you could be back to see us in a tin of German bully beef.'

Occasionally, some of us made small raids on the German positions, generally aiming to return with one or two prisoners. And it was through this that I discovered that the Germans told their own strange stories to their men. I was present when two prisoners who had just been captured were offered a cigarette each. They shrank away in fear. We probed because we instantly knew there had to be something behind their action.

Apparently they had been told that if captured by New Zealanders, they would be given a smoke to lull them into a false sense of security. Then when we had got all the information from them that we could, we would hand them over to our Maori cannibals. They would then be eaten.

At first, our men were hugely indignant to have our Maoris slandered this way. The indignation gave way to laughter. It was a general practice to hand prisoners over to the Maori troops to be escorted to the rear because the Maoris treated them exceptionally well, more like friends than enemies. We eventually and deliberately handed these two prisoners over to two of our Maori troops. We told them the story of what they were supposed to do with the Germans. They all managed a good laugh together.

So much for the propaganda that was given on both sides to make us fight.

During this period, 20 Yank troops were attached to us for experience. Some of their troops had already been in action, and these men were to form a new and untried division as part of the first Yank army being formed.

They were as green as grass. They were eager to be up and doing but ignored all the warnings we gave them. They were obsessed with the idea of being in Berlin in a week. They told us immediately they arrived that they were not here to play rabbits to anyone. We laughed. We suggested otherwise to them. But argument and common sense were useless. We offered to let them find out for themselves.

Because there was very little action and the Yanks could not see dozens of 'Jerries' walking around or waiting to be killed, they formed the opinion that Jerry was a 'damn poor boob of a soldat'. Some of the Yanks had learnt half a dozen words of French since arriving and grasped every opportunity to tell us. It did not take long before I was reacting to their damnable confidence that was only equalled by their colossal ignorance.

One smart Yank became very annoyed at the lack of action and said he would do a little quiet sniping. He disdained the offer of our concealed possies. Very calmly, he pushed his rifle over the parapet, grabbed a periscope and started to have a look. We watched. As we expected, up came the German sniper's dummy. We tried to persuade the Yank that we had known the Germans for a few years now, and this was a Jerry trick. No amount of telling convinced him. To try and finally put him off, we called for a burial party. That, too, failed to stop him. My team turned to leave him to it. We were too disgusted to care what happened. As we moved back, the Yank bobbed up like a jack-in-a-box and grabbed his rifle. There was a sharp crack. It wasn't the Yank's rifle. He was dead, shot right between his eyes. The bullet had, of course, come from a different direction than the dummy.

The Yank's mate, who had encouraged him, got such a scare that for a few minutes he trembled like a leaf in a storm. We suggested he profit from the lesson. But at dusk, we buried him with his mate.

The remaining 18 Yanks soon learnt that a certain kind of

confidence can be a bad thing. They became a rather subdued bunch. We deliberately set all kinds of traps for them to fall into while they were in the trench. They did not take showing or telling twice after the death of their two mates. Some of them became very surly and sullen if they got beaten in any game or activity with us over the next days even when we hadn't set it up. I didn't like this lack of sportsmanship and for this reason they were not very popular.

The aerial combats and regular shelling from both sides were now pitting the countryside with a plentiful array of shell holes. We were kept busy strengthening our defences to the rear.

We thought the push to Paris would certainly be in the minds of the Germans and constantly expected an attack on a grand scale. But it didn't come and didn't come. Being forever on the alert had a great deal to do with our general restlessness and never-ending strain. I would have welcomed any action in preference to just marking time and setting traps for the Yanks.

And right at the time most of us were keyed up to concert pitch with discontent, we were relieved by the Aussies. We were sent back to Vauchelles-les-Authie, south of Authie Wood, about 8 miles from the front. We were to rest and train for another offensive to try and recapture Bapaume.

Vauchelles was like so many small French villages and especially pretty. It was just the sort of place that gave this area of Picardy such a good name for its beauty and peaceful scenes. We were not bothered with shells and most of the area was still under cultivation. From here to Authie Wood, the countryside was a huge sheet of gold when the sun rose across the ripening wheat, oats and barley. It was just splendid to look at.

I fervently hoped that we would be put to harvesting the

crops. I wanted that kind of exercise. But because we were here to train for the Bapaume Stunt, we were, instead, put to treading them down. I couldn't believe it. We ruined about 4000 acres, with no attempt to harvest, just because of the training. I thought at least we could have harvested the crops for the horses. Day after day, we helped to completely ruin all this grain. Our consciences smote many of us, knowing the thousands of hungry mouths the grain would have fed. But we were powerless. We were at manoeuvres from early morning to late afternoon. I don't know where the French farmers had gone. It didn't appear that they had fled. They had had no need to.

We had only been at Vauchelles a few days when Bill Massey, the New Zealand Prime Minister, and Joe Ward, the Opposition leader, arrived. They both looked well, but the tin hat made rather a guy of old Bill. It did not suit his proportions at all. On Sunday, Bill and Joe attended a church parade with us. Church was held on the slope opposite the camp and, in full sunshine, the newly polished instruments of the band were dazzling to my eyes. They gave just that dash of splendour to make the parade an imposing scene.

As soon as the service was over, Bill stood to speak, to be followed by a few words from Joe. It didn't happen. A flight of Gothas, guarded by about a dozen Albatrosses, appeared in the sky. We realised the camp could be their objective and our parade made a tempting target. We scattered, many of us taking to the open grain fields.

It was the end of the parade, unfortunately. Some of us were annoyed. We had one or two pointed questions to ask Bill about the fighting to the 'last man'. But our chance was gone. I liked the two men for coming to see the set-up and what we were involved in. They saw it, even going into the front, and did not just tour the back areas. Old Bill seemed a great man, although I thought his politics all wrong. That was a pity.

The restlessness and the strain led to my becoming carefree. One night we had to be in camp for roll call at 9pm. I ignored it and put in an appearance after 10.30pm. To make matters worse, I was merry. That did not go down well. Next morning, I was up before the CO. I got two days confined to barracks, or CB as we called it.

CB and pack drill had lost any appeal for me that they might ever have had. After attending the two first calls, I sneaked out of camp and to the village. I met up with Lew and together we joined the two-up ring. That night, I could do no wrong. I made over 640 francs, or about £30 pounds, in only a few hours. Ten minutes before closing, Lew bought four bottles of champagne and a bottle of vin blanc for a 'make weight'. We drank well.

We reached camp about 2am. I was hardly able to stand. The vin blanc on top of the champagne had knocked me into a very happy state. Lew decided to sneak in at the rear of the camp. I brazenly walked, as best I could, in through the main entrance. I even knew the guard would be waiting for me. Within minutes, I was in the clink — and probably snoring.

For the next two days from 6am until late, the boys were out of camp on manoeuvres. While they sweltered in the increasing heat, I sat back and slept and read. The colonel had been too busy to deal with me but, on the second night, I was tried. I was given another two days in the clink and docked two days' pay. The colonel gave me a sermon as long as my arm. He began with reminding me that I was the youngest in the battalion yet one of the oldest hands in it. He finished with a twinkle and a grin.

But I didn't finish my punishment in the clink. Next morning, 'flu broke out in the army. Like a mug, I was one of the first to go down with it. I reported sick with a very high temperature and some peculiar symptoms I couldn't make sense of. I was isolated immediately. By evening, there were over 20 of us. The tally was pushed up fast through the night.*

This group of us was transferred to a large farm building inside the village. It had been used before as a billet and had about 40 bunks around the walls. But they were filled in no time. Later that day, we were sent to a hospital somewhere near Amiens. Because of the 'flu, I lost all sense of direction and where I was going. I know I was also sent to a divisional rest camp at Vaumeuill, where I spent a couple of weeks, well away from hostilities.

As I improved from the 'flu, I wandered the area around the rest camp. I visited the large aerodrome, half a mile away, where several giant Handley Page bombers and a few combat machines used to go up for a try out each evening before dark. I easily persuaded the pilots into taking me up for a spin. I loved it. Like most foot-sloggers, I wished in those moments that I was in the RAF. They were a decent crowd of pilots and I enjoyed yarning with them. I wished them all the best in the world and was sorry when I left Vaumeuill.

When I rejoined my troops, they were back under canvas at Authie Wood.

I lasted four days. I knew I was cracking up fast now. I had gone down too quickly and for too long with the 'flu. Part of me was not sorry, but this time I developed ulcerated tonsils. By the time I was sent to the field hospital, my tonsils were so enlarged that I was having difficulty breathing. I began having choking spasms. I was giving a choice of sitting in a chair or being chloroformed. I did not fancy the idea of

---

* This was the Spanish 'flu pandemic, which killed an estimated 15–20 million people worldwide during 1918 and 1919.

choking and perhaps dying while under chloroform. I was sat in a chair, my tonsils were painted with cocaine, and out they came. I coughed frequently and blood spurted everywhere. They stood a Red Cross man beside me to paint the cuts and stop the bleeding when I coughed.

After 48 hours of it, I was so weak that I couldn't raise a hand to anything. Yet at the slightest sound, my head was bounding out of bed. It took a week before I could even swallow custard. Even that brought tears to my eyes with the pain.

I was again sent to the 22nd General Hospital at Camiers on the French coast. I was not pleased. The sound of the German bombers was too much and three times in three days, I had to take to the trenches.

I made up my mind to get out as soon as I could. But it was not an easy job. The Yanks had taken over the hospital and insisted on giving us every opportunity to have a good rest. They told me it was now up to them to give us boys a spell.

For three weeks, I kept telling the doctors that I was as good as gold and ready for a return to my troops. I was finally taken before the head doctor. I was not well, and knew it, but I wanted out from the 22nd General. If I was going to be killed, I at least wanted it to be among mates, not beneath a hospital bed.

The head doctor looked me up and down. Before I could say a word, he ordered me to stand aside until he had seen the remaining men. When it was my turn and I was told to strip to the waist, I knew I was in for the whole works. I was punched, prodded and jabbed all over.

'What's your game?' he asked me.

'What do you mean?' I said.

'You're not anything like well enough to return to your men. So what's the game?'

'I'm fed up being in here. I want to get out of the hospital.'

'How long have you been in France?' he asked.

'Over two and a half years,' I answered.

'Hell, no,' he said. 'You're only a kid.'

That stung me. I retorted angrily, 'Maybe I am, but there's no man in France that can tell me anything I don't know about this game.'

'All right, lad, all right,' he said. 'Don't get annoyed. I never meant it that way.' He looked me up and down again. 'Have you ever been to England?' he asked.

'Apart from training camp, once, on 14 days' leave,' I said.

'Righto,' he said. 'Tonight will make twice.'

I nearly fell flat. I could hardly believe what he had said. And that night it was. Before I knew what was happening, I was on the hospital ship heading for convalescent camp in England.

I kept staring at the water, expecting to get called back ashore any minute. I wasn't.

Chapter 14

Convalescent Camps, 1918

The train trip from Dover to Walton-on-Thames was fast and through the middle of the night.* I finally reached the hospital about 3am. I was shown a bath. It helped the cleanliness but not the seediness. I had to wait unsteadily in the corridor for some time to be told which ward I would be sent to.

When the night sister took me in hand, she fired questions at me without waiting for my reply. She seemed to be in bad humour and her attitude towards me got my goat.

'I see you're not wounded,' she snapped.

'No,' I said quietly, 'just sick.'

She eyed me up and down. 'I don't know why some of my friends couldn't be sent back to England when they become sick,' she said peevishly. 'You late arrivals seem to have all the luck,' she added as an afterthought.

'And have your friends been long in France?' I asked, trying to keep my temper under control.

'A few months, but one has been there nine months,' she replied.

I very nearly exploded at her. Instead, I said, 'Then he'll

---

* Walton-on-Thames was No. 2 New Zealand General Hospital, about 17 miles from London.

be just starting to realise he's in a war. Oh, and by the sound of it, he'll be a conscript,' I said sarcastically. I added with some contempt, 'And no doubt he's a very nice sort of chap.'

The night sister realised with my tone that she had put her foot in something. 'Oh, how long have you been in France?'

I decided not to tell her. 'I don't think it matters,' I said.

For the first time while talking, it dawned on her to examine the card pinned to my army tunic.

'Oh, my gosh, I really do apologise,' she offered.

Suddenly, I fell through space with hands trying to drag me back. I didn't lose consciousness but I hit the floor, feeling very dazed and very tired. Two nurses helped me up. As my wits returned, I heard myself in full flight telling the sister what I thought of her and all her conscript friends. The nurses tried to quieten me. I refused, and went at the sister again until I had fully had my say. The sister disappeared. The nurses marched me off to bed. One of them said that if they hadn't been able to shut me up, at least the old tabby had got what she deserved. They warned me to look out for her as she had a habit of evening things up.

For four days I didn't see the sister. But when she walked me to the operating theatre on the fifth day, she meekly asked if I bore any ill will. I laughed and assured her that I did not. For four days I had been ashamed of my outburst, but I decided not to add anything more.

I did admire the splendid work of all hospital staff under these circumstances and did my best to show it by being as little bother as possible. I preferred to be helpful rather than argumentative. I thought enough had been said.

When I came to from the operation, there was a team of seven devils prodding my throat with hot pokers. But I could swallow and I could breathe. After five days I was allowed up for two hours. I couldn't manage it and crawled back into bed almost immediately. It took another two weeks before I could stay up all day. I was still not allowed to leave the grounds.

Because there was a gramophone in the ward, plenty of records and a piano, I had music around me again. We had a billiard room and ping-pong for the more active. The hospital was only a quarter of a mile from the River Thames. It was near mid-summer, the weather was lovely, and crowds were out enjoying the boating. There was so much gaiety, I found it hard to believe what I had left behind in France. England was supposed to be engaged in a bitter war. The scenes didn't fit.

I tried to relax by idly watching people along the river. I desperately wanted to go for a row, but had been forbidden to succumb to temptation. I was slowly able to walk further and further afield and was rowed up to Trowbridge and Shepperton. I loved the greenness of this countryside, the scent of its flower-laden lanes, and the smell of new hay. With the villages nestling on the river, it was all too gloriously peaceful.

Major Fenwick, the head doctor, offered me a job at the hospital until I was ready to leave.* He had seen my thirst for knowledge on anything medical and had heard my asking the nurses question after question. I cleaned his private office, kept his instruments in good order and made myself available for anything he wanted or would tell me. Dr Fenwick explained at length what he did and even let me study his books on anatomy.

I had once had an ambition to be a doctor but I knew it would not happen. My family lacked money, and I had not been grounded in the necessary education.

---

* Percival Clennell Fenwick, from Christchurch, had been the surgeon-captain of the 2nd New Zealand Contingent during the 1899–1902 South African War, and had served at Gallipoli.

Towards the end of summer, I was sent to the con camp at Hornchurch, about 2½ miles from Romford Station.* I was surprised. It was a lovely camp with everything so neat and clean, well laid out and standing in beautiful grounds. The countryside was a picture of delight to me. I was hopeful that Jenny would soon be able to visit.

The only drill expected of me was to attend physical jerks for half an hour before breakfast. It was compulsory to join several educational classes and these took up most of the day. I enjoyed the scheme and the teachers. They were good at their jobs and encouraged me in everything I wanted to study. But there was quite a crowd of men that simply attended because they had no choice. It seemed such a waste of time here if the opportunity to learn wasn't taken.

Leave was granted daily after classes, and after midday on Sundays, until 10pm. Hornchurch itself and Upminster were pretty villages to visit, but I thought Romford, about the only other place to go to, horribly dull after my second trip. Several country estates belonging to Londoners were nearby. They were grand homes and gardens, and I quickly discovered their prolific apple orchards.

London was only 18 miles away, but a special pass was required and given only for very good reasons. My health had improved greatly and there didn't seem to be much wrong with me. But if I had asked for London leave too often, I knew I would be shifted elsewhere.

I knew my sickness had not been helped because I was sick of the war. So I had made a decision on my arrival at Hornchurch. I intended to fight the war from the English front for a while.

This also enabled Jenny to take a trip into the countryside and visit every Sunday. I paid her expenses. She never took a

* Hornchurch New Zealand Convalescent Hospital specialised in massage and electrical treatment.

penny more than it cost her and I had the devil of a job trying to get her to take even the 2s and 3d return fare.

Each Sunday, we chose a different route for our ramble. I enjoyed these immensely and it was very easy to be with Jenny.

I had told her some of my recent struggle with being on the French front and the bombing. I had said that I thought I was going mad at times. But I had reassured her she had nothing to worry about. She didn't doubt me until on one of our rambles. We were strolling through a field when I saw a peculiar movement in the grass a short distance away. Alert, I grabbed a stick from the ground and dashed into the grass. A beautifully marked yellow and black snake, about 2 feet long, slithered away from me. I smacked it with the stick a few times. I turned to call Jenny. She refused to come near me. As I called again, her look of amazement turned to fright. She began to back away from me. I realised she was dead scared of me and probably thought I had now gone completely mad.

I realised she hadn't seen the snake. I began to laugh until tears rolled down my cheeks as I imagined what my actions must have looked like. I grabbed the dead snake behind its head and lifted it up to show her. If Jenny had been scared of me before, she was now horrified of the snake. When she eventually calmed down, she said she hadn't known snakes lived in England. Neither had I. She relaxed, ran to me and gave me such a hug of relief that I spent the rest of the afternoon looking for more snakes.

Just before my departure from Hornchurch, the nearby flying school for trainees held a sports day, attended by the King. Some of our New Zealand boys formed the guard of honour. Initially, I was disappointed with him. He did not come up to my idea of a King at all. He showed no pomp, no outward display, and he mixed with the crowd as one of us. As I watched him, I began to admire his mild-manneredness as a quality I could learn from. I was becoming much more aware of how I wanted to be.

I was drafted to Codford Con Camp and first given a month's leave.* Naturally, I made for London. I booked in at the club and met Jenny. We headed for Hampstead Heath for some quiet time. I couldn't believe it when we arrived. There were dozens of couples spread everywhere with rugs and picnics. Again, it was such a contrast to the last few years in France.

The next morning, I met up with an Aussie in hospital blues. (Convalescent patients, the 'blue boys', wore a special blue uniform faced with red.) He called himself Tassie. I soon learnt that he was not in the least bit sick, but was AWOL — and had been for some months. He had bought a faked pass for a pound in Petticoat Lane, and renewed it every 28 days. His pass was in good enough order that he had no fear of any red cap pinching him and returning him to his barracks. We teamed up during the days and I met with Jenny at night after she finished work. But after a week, Jenny went down with the 'flu and confined herself to bed. She insisted that after visiting her each day, I now spent my nights with Tassie. It did not take long, and we started getting caught up in mischief.

We were returning to the club after seeing *Chu Chin Chow*, a musical that all troops on leave attended, and walking through Bloomsbury Square, when we heard a cry for help. We saw three figures 50 yards ahead of us struggling violently in what was plainly a robbery. I shouted that I was on my way and drew my Luger pistol as I ran. To attract attention, I fired two shots into the air. Two of the men bolted,

---

* No. 3 New Zealand General Hospital at Codford was only a few miles from Sling Camp.

leaving a rather large West Indian private sprawled on the ground. He had clearly been given a rough handling as I had seen the men putting their boots into him. His face was covered with blood and he was half senseless. I pocketed my Luger and bent over him.

I was knocked flying. A burly copper pounced on me and had me handcuffed before I had time to speak. Like a mad dog, Tassie let fly at the cop. He landed hit after hit on him before being grabbed by two other policemen. By now, I was as mad as Tassie, and started to abuse the cop who had floored me. Tassie added his loud voice to my swearing.

The West Indian revived sufficiently and joined in the swearing at the cops. Eventually, he was able to explain that Tassie and I had saved him, not robbed him. It was music in my ears to hear the police sergeant now swear at the cop who had hit me. We joined back in. Tassie was still wild enough to want to have another go at the cop. The handcuffs were taken off. The sergeant asked who had fired the shots and I produced my pistol. He sniffed at it, satisfied himself and handed it back.

Tassie was very curious to know where I had got the pistol. This one I had taken from a captured German lieutenant at Colincamps. I had taken others and sold them for money to keep me in two-up. Tassie was hurt that I had not told him about the pistol. I had had no reason to mention it and said so. He wanted to buy it from me. I said no, I would not part with it.

As we returned to the club, Tassie didn't speak. I asked him why he was so quiet.

'I wish I owned a pistol like that,' he said. 'By gosh, then things would hum.'

'Hey, in that case,' I said straight to him, 'we'd better part now. There'll be no dirty work, Tassie, while I own it.'

'Sell it to me?' he asked.

'No, I will not. You seem to want it pretty badly. Maybe you'll try and pinch it from me.'

'Listen,' he said, 'you're my mate. If you had a dozen pistols I wouldn't pinch one from you.'

'Okay, I believe you. So, let's shake hands on it. But I want you to understand that I only carry it for defence.'

Nothing more was said about the pistol for a couple of days until Tassie and I were at the Kingsway Theatre. At halftime, he went out for a smoke. I stayed inside. Suddenly, Tassie returned and grabbed my arm.

'Quick,' he said, 'give me your squirt, quick. Grab your hat and coat, follow me to the lavatory.'

I gave him the pistol without a word. From his urgency, I expected there to be a row brewing. I followed, a few yards behind. He made a wild dive for the lavatory door, and stopped halfway through it.

'Oh, it's all over,' he said. He ushered me out. 'Wait for me at the corner, I won't be long. I just want to use it,' he said casually.

I did as he asked and waited at the street corner, barely 50 yards away. He joined me quite quickly and we walked up Southampton Row together. I looked hard at Tassie. There was no sign of excitement about him. I started to feel reassured as I had had some doubts about his hurry.

'Don't ask any questions yet,' he said. 'I'll explain shortly. Please do as I ask.'

All sorts of wild notions went through my head again. But I couldn't do anything with what I didn't know. I followed and did what he wanted. He booked a room for the night at the Salvation Army Hostel on the Row near Russell Square. Tassie took the key and, in silence, we quickly made our way to the room. He locked the door, shot home the bolt, walked over to the window, said 'Good' and turned to me with a grin from ear to ear. My heart began to sink. There was no doubt in my mind he had got up to something.

He handed me the pistol and said, 'That's yours.' He put his hand into his trouser pocket and said, 'And this is ours.' He produced a very large roll of £1 notes and laid them out in front of me. I was stunned. I looked at Tassie but couldn't speak.

He explained that when he had gone to the lavatory, he had seen a civilian counting a roll of money and holding a handful of jewellery. Tassie had immediately thought of the pistol. Getting the pistol and me out of the theatre by bluff was the easy bit. As soon as I headed for the corner, Tassie pointed the pistol at the civilian and told him to give up half of the money or he would lose the lot. The civilian parted with it like a lamb.

'So you see,' added Tassie, 'I only took half of what he had obviously stolen for us.'

'How do I know that's true?' I demanded.

'You'll have to take my word for it.'

'I suppose I will.'

'So the argument's settled.'

I was in no position to know if Tassie's story was right or wrong. He counted the money.

'A hundred and seventeen pounds,' he said. He handed me half.

'I can't touch that. I don't want any stolen money,' I argued.

'Take it,' he insisted. We continued to argue until I finally took £30 from him. Tassie was satisfied. So was I that it was over.

'If anything like this happens again, Tassie, I'm finished with you. I don't want to live like this.'

He agreed. In spite of what he had done, I liked him. I would have been sorry to keep quarrelling. I think Tassie knew that and played on it all he could. I told him that if there were any more of his tricks, though, I would break with him. For the first time, Tassie told me how he had been living for several months by picking pockets and carrying out similar stand-over stunts as he had tonight.

I would have had a short life with Tassie's capers. I was damned glad when Jenny got better. I talked her into taking a week's holiday before she went back to work.

We left London for the Midlands, Liverpool, Leeds and return by the east coast. We continued to Brighton for the last night. Only once when I asked for single rooms each, did I meet an astonished attitude that had taken for granted that Jenny was on overnight girl for me. Both Jenny and I were angry. We expected our relationship to look more than that.

I met up with Tassie on my return. He couldn't wait to show me several wallets he had 'picked'. None contained much. I asked him to cut it out. He laughed and said he had to live somehow. I told him I didn't then care what he did as long as he kept me out of it. I wanted nothing to do with his stealing.

One lovely night after seeing Jenny home, I returned to the club by walking from Canonbury Road to Russell Square instead of taking the tram or tube. I was nearing Holborn and what would be familiar streets when another air-raid warning sounded.

Instantly, every light went out and the bustle for shelters began. I saw no point in rushing for any tube stations as they were usually packed by people who spent every night there, own bedding and all. I turned into Harpur, the next street, looking for a basement. When it looked to be a blind street, I hesitated, wondering what was my best course. It was decided for me.

A tornado in a nightdress and overcoat hit me on my right flank, sprawling me across the footpath. I swore, ready to grab at her. She crouched against the base of a building, shivering, her mouth working spasmodically but without sound. I didn't think this was a case for gentle measures. I dragged her to her feet and insisted on knowing what the hell she meant by knocking me over. I didn't expect an answer and nor did I get one. I shook her as if I were a dog with a rat. Still nothing. I smacked her sharply on her cheek, followed by another and another. She started to whimper. In the next instant, she grabbed me around my throat and tried to strangle me. She might have been small but she was no weakling in her terror.

I broke her hold, turned her around, grabbed both her arms from behind and tried to push her towards a shelter. At exactly the same time, I heard that dreaded 'whoosh, whoosh, whoosh' of a falling bomb. She heard it too. She tried to fight me. I tried to hold her, knowing it would be useless to run. As the bomb exploded nearby with an almighty roar, the girl collapsed in my arms. The sudden withdrawal of her resistance threw me over the top of her. I hit my head on the pavement, sending me dizzy.

A policeman pulled me off her. I almost expected to get handcuffed again, but he said he thought the girl came from a house nearby. I carried her to it and knocked, but other women inside would not come out on to the street. I said I would carry her in and the policeman left me to it and continued his beat.

The women soon brought the girl to, but she was thoroughly exhausted. She did belong in the house and her room was upstairs. As soon as there was no further sound of bombing, I carried her up to her bed. I was about to leave, when she started going hysterical all over again. She trembled like a leaf. I tried to humour her and encourage her to sleep. But she couldn't for some time. The women brought me some whisky for her, but she refused it. She wouldn't let me go. I was stumped as to what to do. In the early hours of the morning, she moved over and invited me to lie down on the bed and sleep. She pulled a blanket over me.

I awoke to the sound of laughter and the women of the house standing beside the bed and in the doorway. I was confused. I was in a strange room with someone beside me and I knew I was fully dressed except for my boots and puttees. I tried to explain but they said I had no need to. They made me breakfast and made me promise to visit again. I did during the days and the women were only too pleased to talk and show me some of the local sights.

Only one bomb had fallen the night I met the girl in Harpur Street. It had exploded on the footpath in Southampton Row, blowing out windows along both sides for about 75 yards but only causing moderate damage to property. The large, double-faced clock that was suspended from the doorway of the Pitman Institute created some unusual interest after the explosion. The face closest to the explosion was intact, while the face furthest away, was damaged. For all of my experience with the effects of bombs, it still took me a couple of minutes to realise how that had happened.

Jenny took me to Petticoat Lane again. As usual on a Sunday, it was packed with crowds haggling and buying. I couldn't believe some of the rubbish that found a market. Jenny had me watch one exchange that epitomised my surprise. A woman bought a bundle of old boot brushes that had next to no bristles left on them. In my ignorance, I thought she was mad to waste even 3d a dozen. Jenny explained that the woman would only want the backs. She would remove the part that held the bristles, put fresh bristles on them, sandpaper the backs, varnish them and resell them as new brushes. In that moment, I understood why so much useless junk was sold from so many useless-looking stalls.

Women ran most of the stalls. We had to be careful how we spoke to them unless looking for trouble. They were very capable of looking after themselves. I heard one of our artillerymen call a woman trying to sell stockings a squawking old hen. She slapped him across his cheek. As he turned to flee, she grabbed a broom handle from another stall and cracked him across the back with it.

It was easy to buy a dozen near perfectly forged Bank of England £1 notes for just £1. Pickpockets were numerous and though I carried my money belt without money in it, I unfortunately lost it without my knowing, even though I admired the clever work. I was just pleased I had kept to my system of carrying as little money with me as possible.

It was common to be pestered by half-drunk soldiers for the loan of a pound or two. It was never less than 10s. To offer 2s and 6d was to unleash a stream of abuse. I decided that the only way to deal with these men was to say that I was on the point of asking them exactly the same thing for the same amount.

Some nights if I got past these men successfully, I was faced with the dozens of prostitutes. Many were worse than the soldier cadgers. I continually had to tell them to go to hell and, for my troubles, would have to hear a barrage of comments blackguarding me right up the street. They didn't seem to care who heard them.

The ladies in the bars were equally as difficult to avoid. It was not expected that we could stand at the bar and have our drink. If I was on my own or with Tassie and I put down an empty glass on a table, a lady would pounce, take my glass to the bar, order another one and one for herself, and invite herself to join me before I almost had a chance to see what was happening. The lady would then dash headlong into talk of France or New Zealand. They were good at pretending how eager they were to learn. If I told them they were not welcome, I would sneeringly be called a 'mama's boy', or told how virtuous I was.

Shame was an unknown quantity. From what I saw, a certain class of the women of England was simply going mad during the war. I often couldn't believe the trickery and schemes they thought of to gain money or put something over us. I thought it gross and disgusting and like a depraved class of people. I just could not imagine going to bed with any of them.

Yet there were the humorous situations that came from the women as well. I was asked if I knew Corporal Jack Otago because the woman had lost his address. I said no. I was told I must, as Jack's father owns Otago and the district was named after him and was the largest in New Zealand. I of course remembered Jack but forgot which regiment. I was asked about the soldier whose father was the owner of the treacle factory on Lambton Quay. I was asked about the soldier whose father was the major shareholder in the walking stick factory on Oriental Bay. I was asked about the soldier whose father was the stonemason at Karori. What amazed me was not the stories from my fellow New Zealanders, but that they were believed.

The most ignorant story I witnessed involved two Maori mates on leave in London. Tassie and I were walking just behind them up the Strand when two girls began trailing the two Maoris, trying to hear what they were talking about. One of the girls turned to the other and suddenly exclaimed that the men spoke English. I burst out laughing. The girl turned on me and indignantly demanded to know if I was laughing at her. I explained that we could all speak English. She apologised, saying that she had felt safe with Tassie and me behind her but had been led to believe that Maoris were still cannibals, unable to speak English.

In fact, I thought our Maori men spoke purer English than most English. In my time in England, I had formed the view that if I wanted to hear poor English spoken, come to England.

When my leave expired, I was not sorry. I had not wanted to leave London while Jenny was here, and even though there had been so much to see, I was now tired of the city. I had become hemmed in. I wanted the open spaces of green fields and clear air.

As I travelled by train to Codford Con Camp, I never took my eyes off the scenery. Everything was clean, fresh and new. I realised how much I needed the countryside. I again made a decision. I was not going to go back to France for at least six months if I could manage it. I might then have stopped jumping inside at every sound, and my breathing might have become regular again.

Codford village was a grubby little hole. There was hardly a redeeming feature to help me find it attractive. A sluggish stream winding behind the camp with a few ducks swimming in it provided the only homely scene in the whole place. I wondered what I had felt so good about leaving London for.

Seventeen camps made up the military layout, supported by three canteens to serve the needs of the troops. In addition, the YMCA and Church of England ran their canteens, and the Salvation Army attended to spiritual needs. Captain Winton was a popular padre. His church was also the picture theatre.

It was his custom to have a rousing singsong each night before the pictures started. He didn't push hymns but every other variety of song we knew. Consequently, the turnouts were huge.

When I lined up at the camp HQ with several others on my arrival, we were asked if there was a cook among us. I took a chance and stepped out front. Four of us were handed over to the chief cook. Fortunately, he asked a few simple questions, found my answers satisfactory and detailed me to No. 14 Camp. The cook in charge took the wind out of my growing sails with his first question.

'Are you a boxer, lad?'

'Hell, no, far from it,' I said.

'Right. We'll train you — first to cook, then to box.'

And they did. They introduced themselves. Ten out of the 12 cooks were boxers. I settled quickly among them and at the end of a month was gazetted as a cook in camp orders. This meant that as long as I behaved myself, I had a job as a cook for as long as I liked. Being gazetted also included an increase of 2s and 6d a day. I didn't really think I needed it. I continued to do so well at two-up whenever I played that I had plenty of money to draw on.

Soon after my arrival at No. 14, the New Zealanders went into training for the army boxing tournament, with Codford the headquarters. Five of the 10 boxers in No. 14 entered. Among them were Fred McFarlane, New Zealand welter champion; Tommy Spearman, New Zealand light champion; Billy Coombes, Opunake district welter; Jack Heeney, Gisborne; and Jack Royal, Wellington heavy. Billy Davis, the former lightweight champion of England, was their trainer.

A spare hut was converted into a gym during our rest time from daily duties. They needed some men to train against. I was one of five mugs. I became a punching ball.

I was nothing else. They took it easy with me and I stuck to it and learnt from them, yet at the end of their first week of training, I was in an awful mess. I was so sore I asked to be a night cook. This meant I worked from 10pm to 6am, with little to do until 4am and breakfast preparation. The training did not interfere with our work and I was able to get in some extra sleep for my weary body. But did I have to work hard at my breathing in that first week.

The Aussies had a large camp at Sutton Veney, 7 miles north. They frequented our camp because of our better canteens or because they were AWOL from drill or because they just wanted to watch the boxing training. Football was also in full swing with the New Zealand camps against each other and collectively against the Aussies. There was some incredibly good-natured and comedic barracking between the Aussies and us. It made for spontaneous and witty afternoons, often assisted with a plentiful supply of beer. It was all fun and no strain. I couldn't believe the different worlds I had found myself in.

Often on a Thursday for my 12 hours' leave, I visited Bath, only 25 miles away. I kept going back because I so enjoyed the old city for its Roman Baths, and the medicinal properties of its mineral water, and for its cafés and markets. It was at one of these fairs that I met Violet, or Vi as I called her. She was an excellent guide, and with her I saw all there was of Bath. I met up with Vi several times, met her parents and liked her company.

The locals of Bath often stopped me on the street in an easy and familiar way to ask questions about New Zealand. There was something special about the manner in which they did this and I was always pleased to tell them what I could. I was very attracted to Bath. I sometimes wondered if it was because I had had so few in the last three years.

Chapter 15

Armistice Remembered, 1930

The announcement of the Armistice is one of those events that is talked about as a moment when we will always remember where each of us was and what each of us was doing.

I sit here among a group of former New Zealand soldiers on this remembrance trip as each of us talks about our Armistice Day memory. When the announcement was made, some were still fighting on the Western Front, some were on leave in London and some were recovering from their war wounds in hospital. One, who was a prisoner behind the German lines, did not know about the Armistice until days afterwards.

Their stories are special. We gasp, hold back tears, say a few words of anger, and even try and burst into a few bars of an old wartime song. For me, though, it was not a profound moment in my army life. I have no reason to return to where I was or to sing out of tune. But my story draws laughter.

The Armistice was signed at 5am, but when all guns stopped at 11am on the 11th November, 1918, I was completing canteen duties while still at Codford Camp.

I remember the camp staying surprisingly quiet during

the day. The night became the direct opposite. The wet canteens had been thrown open to the troops with free beer for all from mid-afternoon. And as evening approached, the shouting, singing and joy over the Armistice increased considerably. But because of the Armistice, all other rations had been stopped after breakfast leaving only enough food for breakfast the next morning. By about 9pm, over 200 of the men had gathered outside the canteen demanding supper. We said that all we could give them was a drink of tea.

It was too much like rations in the trenches. Only there was no mud, no rats, no shelling, and we were in England. The men clamoured for supper. We said that if they gave us time we would cook supper with the breakfast rations but they would have to go without breakfast. The men wanted both. They were understandably very drunk and did not want to see reason over the lack of food. There was no reason for the rations to have been stopped. But the cooks and I had to look after the canteen.

We had the coppers of hot water nearly boiling. Our CO, Captain Foord I think, spoke quickly to us and we prepared a plan of attack of sorts. The CO turned to the men outside and again offered them a drink of tea. The men said no.

'Righto,' said the CO, 'you won't even get tea.'

The men started shouting and threatened to wreck the canteen.

'Give it a go if you have to,' said the CO, 'but I warn you that the first men to rush the place will meet boiling water.'

He threw the doors wide open so that the men could see the boilers bubbling away. And beside each boiler, we had lined up two of the canteen staff holding big ladles over the boiling water, with four more of us, each holding a German automatic or British Army colt .45.

'Come on,' he said, 'any triers?'

The men cursed and swore but drifted away. We all breathed a sigh of relief. If the CO's bluff had failed, we had agreed with him not to lift a finger against the men. We would all bolt together and not stop whatever they did in that mood. It was, after all, Armistice Day.

And then right alongside us, not 50 yards away, the group that had now grown to about 500 demanded the release of all prisoners in the clink. Their demand was turned down flat by Colonel Griffiths, the camp commandant. But things looked simple for the troops and there was no arguing with them. There was no armed guard and only half a dozen red caps. The troops acted quickly. They handcuffed the colonel, the adjutant and the red caps before any of that group knew what was happening. The prisoners, only seven of them, and none there for any serious offence, were released.

The troops replaced them with their new prisoners and securely locked them in. It seemed a fair exchange at that hour of the night. The troops headed back for more free beer.

It didn't take long for the plight of the colonel to be discovered by other officers. They were released but wisely made no effort to round up the legitimate prisoners or to challenge the men.

At the same time in a neighbouring camp, the men, also full of beer, took charge of their dry canteen, wrecked it and looted everything worth taking. The men who were held in the 'barbed wire' camp, those with VD and therefore isolated, were obviously feeling left out of the drunken activities.* They broke loose and lost themselves in the crowds. A group of Aussies stole one of the 5-ton motor lorries but ran it into a ditch before getting to whatever destination they had in mind.

---

* This was the Venereal Disease Section attached to Codford. Many of the men contracted VD while on leave in London.

The mayhem did not settle down until next morning. The colonel called for a general parade. He had a few words about the previous night but was speaking to about half of the number on the rolls of the camp. It didn't seem to matter that the other half were missing. But it did take a few days to find the prisoners. We had to get back into routines.

It quickly became clear that many of us running the camp would still be at Codford until well after Christmas. The camp was expected to continually fill and empty with troops passing through on their way home to New Zealand.

And I remember that Christmas as one the New Zealand Army gave us that we wouldn't forget. They provided all the New Zealand camps in England with lots of extras and luxuries. The cost must have run into thousands of pounds. We cooks worked incredibly hard to make it a success for the 600 of us at Codford. Apart from the ordinary preparations for Christmas dinner, we had the ingredients to cook extra turkeys, pies, pastries and cakes.

And then there were our Christmas puddings and sauce. What a wonderful success a small thing such as a Christmas pudding and its sauce can be — and what it can do to memories.

We made the sauce in a 50-gallon copper. The army supplied us with two bottles of brandy to add to it. Some of us thought this piece of generosity was still not enough. We asked the men for a donation to help us make the best and strongest sauce we could. First one, then another, and another bottle of brandy arrived until we had 14 more, I think. Every drop went into the sauce. At the end of the puddings, needless to say, there was no sauce left. And, I am sure, nearly everyone in camp was pleasantly drunk on our hot brandied sauce. It was enough to send off the best army boozer.

Chapter 16

Return Home, 1919

Eventually, I was placed on a boat list for home, due to leave in April, 1919. I was granted a week's leave before sailing and on the 1st April, I travelled to Bath for a last visit and to see Vi. I bade her, and her family, farewell. The next day I got to London as fast as I could to meet up with Jenny for the rest of my leave. We spent every day and every night together and wandered London visiting anything we hadn't seen before.

Jenny kept persisting, every moment she could, that I get my discharge in England. I wouldn't agree.

I knew I had to return to New Zealand to be discharged there. I wanted to see Mum, and probably Ina, briefly. I had no thoughts that Ina and I would continue seeing each other again, even though I had sent letters and presents when I could. It would be three and a half years since we had seen each other, and she had been living in Wellington during most of that time. I felt very different from the 17-year-old I had been.

While I had been in France, Ina's few letters had developed a tone in them that suggested she had other things in her life. It actually suited me if she had. She would probably have picked up similar things from my letters. But I wrote to let her know I would visit as soon as the boat arrived in Wellington.

I promised Jenny that I would come back to England for her as soon as I had been discharged. We found a small jeweller's shop, selected a gold band, and celebrated my expected return by getting engaged.

From Codford, the train took a large group of us right on to the wharf at Plymouth where we embarked on flat-bottomed lighters to be towed out to the *Rimutaka*, anchored out in the stream. Considering that so many troops had already left, we were still given a great send-off.

Because of rough seas, it took 11 days to cross the Atlantic to Newport News, on the Virginian coast of America, where we were going to be laid up for several days for repairs and to take on coal. As we came up the harbour, I could clearly see the sign hung out for us. 'Oh Boy, Oh Joy, Home Again.' The sign was an immediate cause of jesting and sarcasm from some of us at our fellow American 'soldats'.

We were taken ashore to where the American Red Cross ladies gave us coffee, cakes, cigarettes, cigars and cheers to make us welcome. Their warmth had a few of us feel a little ashamed at some of our earlier remarks.

During our stay in Newport, we were to be accommodated in a camp about 5 miles away. It became another route march, but more relaxed than most I had been on. The locals, black and white, turned out en masse and added to the welcome.

Next day, a special train took about 300 of us to Washington. Our reception in the capital city was nothing short of marvellous. Everyone vied with each other to add their individual touch.

It was only spoilt by a group of American soldiers who showed annoyance at us New Zealanders wearing broad-brimmed felt hats like theirs. They remarked that our hats were American hats only correctly worn by Americans. Their comments got me worked up. I retorted that the same class of hat was worn by New Zealanders both in South Africa and through the war just finished.

I added, 'We've got more right to be proud of ours than you have of yours, Yanks!'

I expected a fight. I was quite willing and ready for it, thinking that I had learnt a few things back in camp with my boxing cooks.

But to my surprise, an American soldier called back, 'Hey, man, I agree with you.' He pointed to the service chevrons on my sleeve and politely asked, 'So just how much service do those represent?'

I displayed my four blue chevrons for everyone in his group and said, 'They're the result of four years' active service, one for each year.' They actually only represented three years' active service, but I was betting to myself that none of them would know that and betting that none of my mates would correct me.

'You're pretty young, lad, for four years' active service,' called out someone in the crowd.

I pulled out my papers and paybooks. I called back, 'Check them if you don't believe me.'

'Well, boy, I guess you're right,' said the soldier. 'You have more claim to your hat than I do mine.'

The crowd around us heard all this and cheered for me.

'Put away your papers, lad, put 'em away and let's get busy on other things,' they shouted.

I took their advice.

Before I knew it, I was whisked into a private car and taken around the city with four guides at my command. Eight hours later they returned me to the train. I had spent half a dollar for a drink for the party and was only allowed to do that after a friendly argument.

It had been a great day in which time simply flew. At the station, we exchanged addresses and promises to write. I mightn't have changed my view of the Yankee 'soldat' but I now had a different view of his hospitality.

Over the next few days, wherever we went, we were showered with lots of invitations, many for just a chat and a cup of tea. I accepted as many as was possible. These Americans expressed great interest in us individually as well as in New Zealand. So few had known anything of New Zealand and we were the first troops to stay more than 24 hours.

Several of my mates and I even spent a day and evening being hosted to a picnic and a party in the lovely and large home of a prosperous business family. I parted with another standing invitation to call if I ever returned. I took with me a very high regard for them. (I actually wrote to this family for about four years before we lost touch with each other.)

When we sailed through the Panama Canal, I became sick and dazed, and for a few days I did not feel very good at all. I thought I had spent enough time convalescing. I only began to feel better as we reached Pitcairn Island, where we paused to barter for fruit and vegetables from the boats that greeted us. I had a long yarn with some of them across the water between our boats, and especially became interested in the Young brothers who were the direct descendants of the skipper of the mutineers. As we sailed from their fascinating harbour, they sang in splendid harmony, 'God be with you till we meet again'.

As we sailed closer and closer to New Zealand, many of us got caught up in favourite songs. One of the most rousing that suited the circumstances also brought out a lot of our fears for what we would find.

> *I'm going back to the girl I left behind,*
> *Hope I don't find she's changed her mind,*
> *She whispered to me through her tears*
> *That she would wait for years and years.*
> *Come on then boys, now all together, when I get back*
> *Ring out those wedding bells and ring them till they crack,*
> *I'm just mad about her, cannot live without her,*
> *I'm going back to the girl I left behind.*

Finally, on 29th May 1919, we reached Wellington Harbour just at dark. We anchored in the stream and began the formalities for berthing next morning.

About 11am, which seemed to be the significant hour, we strode off the boat to an enthusiastic welcome. I wanted to get out of the crowd as quickly as I could and headed to Thorndon Station to find out when trains left for Palmerston North. I had time in which to visit Ina. Her address was not far from the station.

I stared at her house. I felt easy about what would probably result but I did not want to make any mistakes and take anything for granted, either way. The only quandary I felt was whether I should knock on the front or back door. I decided to walk down the side of the house to the back in case there were any prying neighbours. It may have been a wise choice.

Ina opened the door to my knock. She grinned and flew into my arms. I started to wonder if I had been foolish in my doubts and for just a moment they, and my engagement to Jenny, vanished.

Suddenly, a replica of Ina, somewhere between two and

three years old, toddled up behind her and called, 'Mum, Mum.' I was momentarily dismayed. But all I could see was a sweet wee kid. I fell for her instantly and picked her up.

Ina led me inside. She told me straight away that she had married. As if to emphasise her information, she went to her bedroom and fetched a baby, only a few months old. It was another delightful-looking daughter.

Ina apologised for almost throwing herself at me. She told me that she was not particularly happy in her marriage and perhaps she had acted in a moment of weakness on seeing me. We chatted for a while about her children. I didn't want to tell her much at all about me as there wouldn't have been any point to it.

I stood to go. Ina took a parcel from a cupboard and gave it to me. She asked me not to open it until I reached home. I immediately guessed that it contained all the gifts I had sent her. I refused to take it and said no, they were hers to do with what she wanted.

I walked slowly back to the station. It felt strange, but instead of being annoyed in any way, I felt glad. It was as if a huge relief had come off my shoulders. I never saw Ina after that.

As I headed by train to Palmerston North, I knew inside myself that I was not in good health. I also knew that it had nothing to do with my visit to Ina. I quietly studied my army papers. Among them were the reminders from the doctors at Codford Convalescent Camp and from the doctor on board the *Rimutaka* to report to the military ward at the nearest public hospital the day after I arrived home.

Mum met me at Palmerston North Station that evening with a lovely welcome and a grand drive home by car. But I was fast not caring about any more welcomes. We talked into the night but I quickly tired under her barrage of questions.

I dropped what must have been my own bomb at her when I said I had to report to hospital. All I was prepared to tell her was that I had been badly gassed, that I continued to suffer from concussion as a result of the shelling at Ypres in 1917, and I kept getting sick too often.

And my 21st birthday, in a few days time, was another that Mum would not get to celebrate with me.

I was told that I would spend the next nine weeks as an in-patient of the Palmerston North Public Hospital. I guessed that I would probably have to spend some time also as an out-patient. I wrote to Jenny as soon as I was admitted to tell her how long I might be.

About a month later, I received a letter from her. It enclosed a ring. She said that she had since met an Aussie whom she liked more than me.

Several weeks later, Jenny wrote to me again. She said that the Aussie turned out to be a total dud, had led her on with a pack of lies, and had left her in the lurch. I was never able to answer her letter. And I never heard again from her.

The Hospital told me that I would have to spend another eleven weeks as an out-patient, reporting weekly. I decided I had had enough. I asked for my discharge.

Like everyone else, I was given a free pass over any railway line throughout New Zealand for the next 28 days. I took the pass and wore my army uniform for one more month. And the month gave me all the time I needed to think back over the last few years.

While I was in hospital and on my train travels, when anyone spoke to me about the war, it was like a red rag to a bull. I was sick of not being well and I was fed up with the whole outfit of the army.

Almost every moment, I struggled with my breathing from being gassed. Almost every day, I suffered concussion from the shelling. I defended any action of my mates and myself but I had no feelings of pride for the way we soldiers had been treated. I had no feelings of pride for being called a crack shot and killing man after man. I had lost mates, shot or blown to pieces beside me. By the time I was sent to Codford Camp, I hardly knew any of the men fighting on the front. My mates were those I met in the moment.

I had met women who left me feeling ashamed of myself. I had met women whom I thought I had a future with, yet they seemed to have lived just for their own moment. I thought of the trenches and mud and pieces of mates' bodies. I thought of a baby tugging at the sleeve of her young mother, and both grinning as I took the baby in my arms. I thought of a dead baby in her dead mother's arms beneath a rough mound of earth that was probably now obliterated.

I wanted to forget it all. I was on my own and I had to rely on me. It seemed as simple as that. I made some decisions.

On the evening of the 28th day of my train tripping, I deliberately put aside my pocket book of notes and carefully folded up my army uniform. I put the uniform alongside everything else I had kept that reminded me of the army and the war. I put the lot under the copper at home. I hesitated just once. For no reason and every reason, I removed my boots. I gave the rest a liberal dose of kerosene. I did not sit in front of it for long. I applied a match and gladly watched it burn.

Chapter 17

1930

It is 1930. I have just returned from a trip to France and Belgium with some former soldiers. For the first time in over 10 years, I talked a little about my sadness and anger at what we are calling the Great War.

I was persuaded to write my remembrances into a journal.

For a while, I didn't know how to start. Accidentally, I found two cablegrams my mother kept among her possessions.

The night I arrived home in 1919, I remember her saying that she had wept every day after the first cablegram. And when she got the second, she said she wept all over again for every one of those days.

I stare at the cablegrams now.

The first, official and from the New Zealand Army, reports my death. It says I was killed in the course of action on 7th June, 1917.

The second cablegram looks less official. It is from me, dated two weeks later. It reports that I am still alive.

They draw a smile.

Epilogue

When I set out to turn Len Coley's journal into a readable story, I knew little more than the names of the Battles of Messines, Ypres and Passchendaele. War history is not a passion of mine, but I had heard something of the Somme, seen by many in almost the same light as Gallipoli, and I had gained some appreciation of Ypres as a symbol of inhumane destruction. I became captivated, and appalled, by Len's descriptions.

It was clear that, for our New Zealand troops at Ypres, October 1917 was a period of both sudden success and devastating sacrifice. Len was involved in the achievements of 4 October; he survived the battle that saw the slaughter of so many New Zealand men in the days that followed. But he had not, as I would have expected, written as much about the attack on Passchendaele Ridge on 12 October. I was curious as to why not.

I was able to confirm that Len's unit, 2nd Wellington, was in the reserves on that day. Len's descriptions leading up to the 12th suggest that he was aware of the potential for a disaster. I did not fully understand how much of a disaster until I began my research. I discovered that the events of October 1917 have not been well embedded in either our history or our folklore, and I was shocked to realise the extent to which our New Zealand troops were sacrificed for a few metres of territory.

The British command had decided to launch a major offensive in Flanders in 1917 to claim the sort of victory that would end the war. The Ypres Salient was to be the focus. If successful, it would lead to the securing of the channel ports and Belgian coastline. The attack in June at Messines (in which Len was injured and presumed dead) was the beginning of that move, which pushed the Germans further back than they had been for two years. By the time Len returned to the front at Ypres, his mates were being prepared for the next stage in the assault.

The surrounding area of Ypres was a disadvantage for the British armies. All the high ground, albeit rises and ridges rather than hills, and including Passchendaele, was in German hands. Because it was close to sea level, the terrain of Flanders had a high water table and it was crossed by a series of ditches and canals. In short, the Allies were on wet and low ground. The weather in October 1917 could not have been worse. There was more than twice the usual rainfall during that time and the ground was a quagmire, destroyed by millions of shells already fired in that region. Just by being there without even attacking, the British were suffering around 7000 casualties a week. The New Zealand Division was already seen by the British Command as an effective attacking force. These troops had been out of the front line since Messines. They were being asked once again 'to go over the top'.

On 4 October, the division secured all its objectives. It dealt successfully with the counter-attacks. It advanced nearly 2000 metres, causing several thousand casualties among the Germans. The New Zealand casualties numbered just over 300 dead and 1300 injured, with about 200 listed as missing.

This casualty rate was still about 25 per cent. The Australians suffered a similar percentage loss. But the combined attack drove the Germans from some vital ground. They were dealt a huge blow and — unknown to the Allies at the time but discovered later — had considered a general withdrawal from beyond the range of the Allied artillery.

New Zealand newspaper reports at the time described the attack as 'the turning point of the war', 'the New Zealanders' greatest and most glorious day', and 'rivalling Wolfe's ascent to the plain of Quebec'.

The New Zealand Division's attack at Passchendaele on 12 October was probably this country's worst-ever military disaster, yet it was under-reported in the New Zealand press compared with the coverage of 4 October. Perhaps it was too big a disaster to report on. The Germans had consolidated and rewired their line, and they held it. The weather was atrocious. The casualty rate for the New Zealand Division was around 60 per cent and as high as 85 per cent in some units. The attack should never have gone ahead. It became the New Zealand Division's one large-scale failure in Belgium, and the morale among the men dropped dramatically. Len's journal picks up that feeling. He may well have understood that his survival was due in part to not fighting on the 12th because he and his mates had fought so well on the 4th.

Between late October and early November, the Canadians secured the last of the high ground, but also at huge cost. In the months that followed, various smaller attacks involving New Zealand troops held the ground they had 'won'. But the extent of the disaster for the New Zealand Division at Passchendaele was eventually described as the nadir of its fortunes, similar to that suffered at Monte Cassino in March 1944 (where, incidentally, another of my uncles fought and was injured).

From July to November 1917 the fighting around Ypres was estimated to have cost the British divisions (including the New Zealand Division) 275,000 casualties, of whom 70,000 were killed. The German figures were similar. It has been estimated that 40,000 men went missing in the mud.

Over the length of the Western Front, the Germans lost 770,000 killed, and the Allied Forces lost 900,000 killed.

Some Further Reading

Glyn Harper, *Massacre at Passchendaele: The New Zealand Story*, HarperCollins, Auckland, 2000.

Glyn Harper, *Spring Offensive: New Zealand and the Second Battle of the Somme*, HarperCollins, Auckland, 2003.

Ben Macintyre, *A Foreign Field: A true story of love and betrayal in the Great War*, HarperCollins, London, 2001.

Nigel Steel and Peter Hart, *Passchendaele: The Sacrificial Ground*, Cassell Military Paperbacks, Cassell, London, 2000.